Learn Spanish for Adult Beginners

Speak Confidently & Impress Your Amigos
A No-Nonsense Guide to Quickly Learn
Vocabulary, Common Phrases, and Master
Pronunciation

Sol Mancilla

© **Copyright 2023: All rights reserved.**

The content contained within this book may not be reproduced, duplicated or transmitted without direct written permission from the author or the publisher.

Under no circumstances will any blame or legal responsibility be held against the publisher, or author, for any damages, reparation, or monetary loss due to the information contained within this book, either directly or indirectly.

Legal Notice:

This book is copyright protected. It is only for personal use. You cannot amend, distribute, sell, use, quote or paraphrase any part, or the content within this book, without the consent of the author or publisher.

Disclaimer Notice:

Please note the information contained within this document is for educational and entertainment purposes only. All effort has been executed to present accurate, up to date, reliable, complete information. No warranties of any kind are declared or implied. Readers acknowledge that the author is not engaged in the rendering of legal, financial, medical or professional advice. The content within this book has been derived from various sources. Please consult a licensed professional before attempting any techniques outlined in this book.

By reading this document, the reader agrees that under no circumstances is the author responsible for any losses, direct or indirect, that are incurred as a result of the use of the information contained within this document, including, but not limited to, errors, omissions, or inaccuracies.

CONTENTS

Introduction   7

1. THE SPANISH ALPHABET AND PRONUNCIATION   15
   The 27 Letters of the Spanish Alphabet   16
   Syllables and Spanish Pronunciation Rules   18
   Understanding the Accent   22
   Common Mistakes With Spanish Pronunciation   23
   5 Tips to Sound More Natural   25
   Practice and Vocabulary   29

2. ESSENTIAL SPANISH VOCABULARY   33
   Colors, Shapes, and Sizes   35
   The Human Body   37
   Clothes and Accessories   38
   Family and Relationships   40
   Around the Home   41
   Travel and Transport   43
   Jobs and the Office   45
   School Subjects   48
   Domestic Chores   49
   Animals   50
   Hobbies   52
   Practice and Vocabulary   53

3. NUMBERS AND TIME   57
   Cardinal and Ordinal Numbers   58
   Telling the Time   61
   Days, Months, and Seasons   63
   Talking About the Weather   64
   Adverbs of Time   66
   Practice and Vocabulary   67

4. COMMON WORDS AND PHRASES FOR
   EVERYDAY SITUATIONS ... 73
   First Impressions ... 75
   Asking and Answering Questions ... 78
   Ordering Food and Drinks ... 80
   Making Reservations and Appointments ... 87
   Money Matters ... 89
   Punctuation Symbols for Email Addresses ... 91
   Expressing Likes and Dislikes ... 92
   Practice and Vocabulary ... 94

5. GETTING COMFORTABLE WITH SPANISH
   GRAMMAR ... 99
   Pronouns ... 99
   Nouns, Their Plurals, and Articles ... 103
   Nouns and Genders That Don't Follow the
   Rules ... 104
   Adjectives ... 105
   Prepositions ... 107
   Basic Sentence Structure ... 110
   Practice and Vocabulary ... 112

6. EVERY SENTENCE NEEDS A VERB ... 125
   Regular Verbs in Spanish ... 126
   "Ser" and "Estar" ... 129
   Irregular Verbs ... 131
   The Simple Tenses ... 135
   The Progressive Tenses ... 144
   Tener: Verb and Phrases ... 148
   The Perfect Tenses ... 150
   Reflexive Verbs ... 153
   Practice and Vocabulary ... 157

7. SPANISH CULTURE AND CUSTOMS ... 177
   Spanish Accents and Dialects ... 178
   How Spanish-Speaking Countries Vary ... 181
   Tips on Navigating Cultural Differences ... 184
   Getting Good at Cultural Immersion ... 186
   Practice and Vocabulary ... 188

BONUS: THE ULTIMATE SECRET TO
MASTERING SPANISH PRONUNCIATION   197
Bonus: Practice and Vocabulary   202

Conclusion   211
References   217

INTRODUCTION

Language is power, life and the instrument of culture, the instrument of domination and liberation.

— ANGELA CARTER

Hola amigos! Have you ever been in a situation where you've found yourself completely lost in a conversation because of a language barrier? Maybe you thought you understood what was being said, only to realize later that you missed a key phrase or expression. This can be frustrating, embarrassing, and even comical at times. Trust me, I've been there!

Years ago, I was introducing some English friends to some Spanish friends, and we all attempted to have a conversation with the help of some translations. However, when one of my Spanish friends used the expression "Donde Jesús perdió su merchero—Where Jesus lost his lighter—" (this phrase refers to a very remote and distant place), my English friends were completely lost. Their confused expressions made me realize that even the most basic phrases and expressions can be a challenge for someone learning a new language.

But fear not, my dear friends, for there is a solution! Learning a new language may seem intimidating, but it will also be one of the most rewarding experiences you can have. With the right tools and approach, you will gain a solid understanding of a new language and open doors to new cultures and experiences. That's why I'm excited to share with you my book, which will provide you with a fun and engaging way to learn Spanish. So, grab a cup of coffee, pull up a chair, and let's get started on this exciting journey together!

Maybe you need to learn Spanish for work and the pressure is blocking you from making any headway. Or perhaps you dream of traveling to Spanish-speaking countries but feel overwhelmed by all the vocabulary and grammar. It's okay, I understand your sorrow.

You're tired of old-school learning techniques like repeating a word over and over again. You want to learn different styles to improve your skills with a range of activities. You're probably thinking back to learning a language at school and how difficult it was. And now you're concerned about trying to understand different dialects and whether others will still understand you. You're constantly translating phrases, and the closest you've gotten to speaking Spanish is essentially a sitcom-styled "Spanglish."

But don't worry, I've got your back. This book is designed to help you overcome these common obstacles and learn Spanish with ease. You'll discover a whole new approach to learning that's engaging, practical, and most importantly, fun.

With my book, you'll gain a solid understanding of the foundations of Spanish, including a wide range of vocabulary, simple grammar rules, and sentence structure. Unlike other solutions, this book will challenge your brain in a fun way, leading to faster results and encouraging you to keep learning more. By the end of these pages, you'll feel certain about your understanding and have the confidence to start conversations with others, opening up a world of new opportunities.

So, whether you need Spanish for work or travel, this is the book for you. Say goodbye to frustration and hello to fluency!

As a language enthusiast, I know the struggle of trying to learn a new language. It can be daunting and frustrating, especially when you don't know where to start or how to continue. That's why I wrote this book: to be the catalyst that will trigger your desire to learn Spanish and provide you with the tools you need to succeed.

If you're reading this, chances are you're already aware of the benefits of learning Spanish. It's the second-largest language spoken by natives and the fourth most spoken language in the world. Being able to speak Spanish allows you to communicate with millions of people, both in your own community and around the world. You could unlock a whole new world of opportunities—from traveling to Spanish-speaking countries and experiencing their culture firsthand, to building new relationships and connections with people from different backgrounds.

But let's face it, learning a language is not easy. It takes dedication, patience, and a lot of hard work. That's where this book comes in. I want to make learning Spanish fun and enjoyable, rather than a chore. With a focus on practical conversation and real-world situations, you'll learn this wonderfully rich language and be able to use it in your everyday life.

No matter if you're a complete beginner or have some previous experience with Spanish, throughout these pages, I will provide you with a solid foundation of vocabulary, grammar, and sentence structure. And with a little bit of effort and practice, you'll soon be able to hold conversations with confidence and ease.

With my experience-proven methods and strategies, you'll be speaking Spanish in no time. No more tedious grammar drills or boring vocabulary lists. Instead, I offer a fun and engaging way to learn Spanish that will challenge your brain and make learning a breeze.

I've accumulated years of experience and knowledge to provide you with a solid understanding of the foundations of Spanish. And the best part? These methods are designed to help you learn faster! You won't be bogged down by lengthy explanations or confusing verb conjugations. Instead, I'll teach you the most essential aspects of the language that you need to know to start speaking with confidence.

This is not just about learning Spanish, it's about immersing yourself in the rich culture behind the language. You'll gain a deep appreciation for Spanish culture and be able to connect with Spanish-speaking communities in a meaningful way.

Now, let me paint a vivid picture of the end result you will achieve by reading this book: Imagine confidently walking into a room full of Spanish-speaking individuals and not only being able to understand everything they're saying but also being able to hold a conversation with them. Think about the new connections and opportunities that would open up for you! From ordering food at a restaurant to making new friends on your next trip to a Spanish-speaking country, the possibilities are endless.

And who better to guide you on this journey than a native Spanish speaker, like myself? I have spent 20 years living in South America and have immersed myself in the regional differences in the language. I have a passion for teaching and helping others gain the benefits of speaking two languages.

Think back to the days before the internet, before apps and language software, before easy access to foreign films and music. Learning a new language was a slow and frustrating process, and many people gave up before achieving any real proficiency.

But times have changed, and the new era of language learning is here. In this book, I'm going to reveal the secrets of how to learn Spanish quickly and easily, without the frustration and confusion of traditional methods.

It wasn't always this easy. When I was first learning English, I struggled to make sense of the complex grammar and pronunciation rules. I felt like I was making no progress, and I was beginning to think that I would never be able to speak the language fluently.

But then, I discovered some new techniques and resources that changed everything. I learned how to focus on the most important vocabulary and grammar structures, how to immerse myself in the language and culture, and how to practice speaking with native speakers.

Now, I'm excited to share these techniques with you. With this book, you'll be able to achieve the promised result of speaking Spanish fluently and confidently. You'll learn how to pronounce every word, how to use practical vocabulary and phrases for everyday communication, and how to appreciate the prosperous and astonishing culture of Spanish-speaking countries.

So, don't give up on your dream of learning Spanish. The new era of language learning is here, and it's easier and more accessible than ever before. Let's get started—and soon enough you'll be ready to impress your amigos with your newfound Spanish skills!

¡Vamos a empezar!

1

THE SPANISH ALPHABET AND PRONUNCIATION

Are you ready to dive into the exciting world of Spanish? Before we start stringing words together to form sentences, we need to master the basics. One of the most fundamental aspects of learning Spanish is understanding the alphabet and how to pronounce each letter correctly.

The great news is that, unlike English, Spanish has a very consistent and logical system of pronunciation. Each letter is pronounced exactly as it is written, with no unexpected surprises or tricky letters to trip you up. So, let's get started on our journey to mastering the Spanish alphabet!

THE 27 LETTERS OF THE SPANISH ALPHABET

Firstly, it's important to know that the Spanish alphabet has the same 26 letters as the English alphabet, plus one additional letter, the ñ. This letter, which is pronounced "eh-nyeh," is used to represent a unique sound in the Spanish language.

To begin our journey, let's take a look at each letter of the Spanish alphabet and how to pronounce it correctly:

- **A** (ah): as in "hola (oh-lah)": hello
- **B** (beh): as in "baño (bah-nyoh)": bathroom
- **C** (ceh): as in "casa (kah-sah)": house
- **CH** (cheh): as in "mucho (moo-cho)": a lot/much
- **D** (deh): as in "deporte (deh-por-teh)": sport
- **E** (eh): as in "leche (leh-cheh)": milk
- **F** (eh-feh): as in "familia (fah-mee-lee-ah)": family
- **G** (heh): as in "gato (gah-toh)": cat
- **H** (a-cheh): as in "huevo (weh-boh)": egg
- **I** (ee): as in "isla (ee-slah)": island
- **J** (ho-tah): as in "jamón (hah-mohn)": ham
- **K** (kah): as in "karaoke (kah-rah-oh-keh)": karaoke
- **L** (eh-leh): as in "luna (loo-nah)": moon
- **LL** (eh-yeh): as in "llave (yah-beh)": key
- **M** (eh-meh): as in "manzana (mahn-sah-nah)": apple
- **N** (eh-neh): as in "nube (noo-beh)": cloud
- **Ñ** (eh-nyeh): as in "mañana (mah-nyah-nah)": morning

- **O** (oh): as in "hola (oh-lah)": hello
- **P** (peh): as in "perro (peh-roh)": dog
- **Q** (kuh): as in "queso (keh-soh)": cheese
- **R** (eh-reh): as in "ratón (rah-tohn)": mouse
- **RR** (eh-rreh): as in "arroz (ah-rrohz)": rice
- **S** (eh-seh): as in "sol (sohl)": sun
- **T** (teh): as in "tren (trehn)": train
- **U** (oo): as in "uno (oo-noh)": one
- **V** (oo-veh): as in "vaca (bah-kah)": cow
- **W** (doh-bleh veh): as in "wifi (wai-fai)": Wi-Fi
- **X** (eh-kees): as in "excusa (ehks-koo-sah)": excuse
- **Y** (yeh): as in "yogur (yoh-goor)": yogurt
- **Z** (zeh-tah): as in "zapato (sah-pah-toh)": shoe

You may have noticed that there are more than 27 letters in this list. That's because, in Spanish, there are 3 compound letters: "ch," "ll," and "rr." The first is known to English speakers in words like "chips" or "chain." We'll discuss "ll" and "rr" later on.

It's essential to take the time to learn and practice the correct pronunciation of each letter to build a strong foundation in Spanish. This will not only help you to pronounce words correctly but also make it easier to understand native Spanish speakers.

It is likely that simply by reading the name of these letters you are not using the correct pronunciation. Don't worry, it's normal. As an English speaker, your brain associates the letters you see with certain sounds. To learn Spanish—or any other language—you will have to build new associations between letters and sounds. I recommend that you check out this Busuu video, available on YouTube, which is super didactic and will help you understand the correct pronunciation of each letter in the Spanish alphabet: Spanish Alphabet: A Simple Guide for English Speakers

As a beginner, you may find Spanish pronunciation a bit challenging, but don't worry, I will make it easy for you to understand.

SYLLABLES AND SPANISH PRONUNCIATION RULES

One of the essential elements of Spanish pronunciation is syllables. In Spanish, most syllables end with a vowel: "ma-má" (mom), "pa-pe-les"(papers), and "a-mi-go" (friend).

Another important rule is that when there is a consonant between two vowels, it forms a syllable with the second vowel. For example, "ca-sa" (house), "pe-rro" (dog), "fa-mi-lia" (family).

It's also essential to understand the difference between strong and weak vowels. Strong vowels include "a," "e," and "o," while weak vowels include "i" and "u." When there is a combination of strong and weak vowels, the weak vowel will often blend in with the strong vowel. For example, "ai-re" (air), "hue-vo" (egg), and "mue-ble" (furniture).

Some consonants aren't separated, meaning they need to be pronounced together as one sound. These consonants include "ch," "ll," "rr," "gu," and "qu." For example, "cho-co-la-te," "lla-ma-da" (call), "a-rroz" (rice), "gue-rra" (war), and "que-so" (cheese).

When two consonants appear together, the first consonant is usually grouped with the preceding vowel, and the second consonant is grouped with the following vowel. For example, "planta" (plant) is divided into "plan-ta" and "apto" is "ap-to" (suitable).

For words with three or more consonants in a row, the rules become so complicated and tedious that most native Spanish speakers don't even know about them. But don't worry, over time you will develop the intuition necessary to separate into syllables, even without remembering the rules by heart. Don't worry about the meaning of the following list of words for now; some are quite advanced! Just focus on trying to learn how the words are separated by syllables.

Here, I leave you a list of words separated into syllables so that you become familiar with them:

- abstracto: abs-trac-to (abstract)
- abstraer: abs-tra-er (to abstract)
- substraer: subs-tra-er (to subtract)
- transplantar: trans-plan-tar (to transplant)
- demonstrar: de-mons-trar (to demonstrate)
- monstruo: mons-truo (monster)

- inscrutable: ins-cru-ta-ble (inscrutable)
- contracciones: con-trac-cio-nes (contractions)
- adscrito: ads-cri-to (assigned)
- circunscribir: cir-cuns-cri-bir (to circumscribe)

Lastly, it's important to understand that prefixes are syllables on their own. For example, "pre-his-tó-ri-co" (prehistoric), "pos-par-to" (postpartum), and "re-to-mar" (resume).

Let's explore the fascinating world of pronunciation in the Spanish language, where a set of rules govern the way words are spoken and sounds are produced. Understanding these rules is key to mastering the art of speaking Spanish fluently and accurately.

In Spanish, the letter "c" is pronounced differently depending on the vowel that follows it. When "c" is followed by an "a," "o," or "u," it is pronounced like the English "k" sound, as in the word "casa." However, when it is followed by an "e" or "i," it is pronounced like the English "s" sound, as in the word "celeste."

Let me show you some examples:

- cielo (cee-eh-loh): sky
- cámara (kah-mah-rah): camera
- césped (sehs-pehd): grass
- culpa (khul-pah): guilt
- correo (ko-rreh-oh): mail

Similarly, the letter "g" in Spanish has two different sounds. When "g" is followed by an "a," "o," or "u," it is pronounced like the English "g" sound, as in the word "gangster" or "gum." However, when "g" is followed by an "e" or "i," it is pronounced like the Spanish "j", with a stronger guttural sound, like imitating an angry kitty; or like a stronger English "h" in "hammer." Here you have some examples:

- goma (goh-mah): eraser
- gafas (gah-fahs): glasses
- gemelo (heh-meh-loh): twin
- gusto (guhs-toh): taste

When it comes to words that contain "gu," we must be careful since there are two special cases. If the "gu" is followed by an "e" or "i," the "u" won't be pronounced, but the "g" sound will still be soft. This rule also applies to many words in English like "guess" or "guillotine." Let me bring you some examples in Spanish:

- guitarra (ghee-tah-rrah): guitar
- guerra (gheh-rrah): war

It is important to mention that in Spanish, the "r" has a soft sound when it is between two vowels as well as at the end of words. For example: "pera" or "motor." In contrast, "r" has a rolling sound when it appears at the beginning of a word. For example: "rosa," "rompecabezas," or "roto." It is also pronounced rolling the "r" when it appears after the consonants "l", "n", and "s." For example: "alrededor" and "enredado."

Understanding these basic Spanish pronunciation rules will give you a strong base to build upon. Don't worry if it takes some time to master them. With practice and patience, you'll be on your way to speaking Spanish like a pro really soon!

UNDERSTANDING THE ACCENT

One of the most important aspects of speaking Spanish correctly is knowing how to use accents or tildes. These little lines over vowels are not just for decoration—they actually play a crucial role in conveying meaning. For example, the word "papá" (with an accent over the second a) means "dad," while "papa" (without the accent) means "potato." As you can see, accents can change the meaning of a word entirely, so it's important to know how to use them correctly.

To help you with this, here are **four rules for using Spanish tildes**:

- Tildes are used to indicate where the stress falls in a word. In general, if a word ends in a vowel, n, or s, the stress will fall on the next-to-last syllable. If it ends in any other letter, the stress will fall on the last syllable.
- Words that do not follow the above rule will have a tilde over the stressed vowel. For example, the word

"árbol" (tree) has a tilde over the first syllable because that's where the stress falls.
- Tildes are used to distinguish between words that are spelled the same but have different meanings. For example, "si" means "if," while "sí" (with a tilde) means "yes."
- Finally, tildes are used in certain interrogative and exclamatory words to indicate emphasis. For example, "¡qué rico!" means "How delicious!"

By following these rules, you will be able to use accents correctly and avoid any confusion when speaking Spanish. So, practice these rules until you feel comfortable using them.

COMMON MISTAKES WITH SPANISH PRONUNCIATION

Let's now address some common mistakes that native English speakers make when pronouncing Spanish words. My experience taught me there are five common pronunciation errors, including mispronouncing the letter "r," pronouncing the letter "h" like the English "h," mispronouncing the letter "j," and confusing the pronunciation of "y" and "ll." These mistakes can often lead to confusion or even hilarity, as in the movie *Spanglish*, when Tea Leoni struggled with rolling the letter "r" while trying to say the name Flor.

- The rolling "r" sound is perhaps the most challenging for English speakers to master, but don't worry, with practice and patience, you'll get there! One tip is to place your tongue at the roof of your mouth and vibrate it as you exhale. It may feel awkward at first, but keep practicing, and you'll soon be rolling your "r"s like a native Spanish speaker.
- Unlike English, the letter "h" in Spanish is silent. That is, it has no sound. When a word contains "h," you just don't pronounce it. For example, "huevo" (egg), is pronounced "weh-boh."
- In Spanish, the letter "j" is pronounced differently than in English. It has a strong sound, similar to the "kh" sound in some Arabic or Hebrew words. This sound is created by forcefully pushing air through the back of the throat while holding the tongue freely without touching the roof of the mouth or teeth like you're about to spit. It's important to note that the "j" sound in Spanish is not the same as the "h" sound, which is silent in Spanish. For instance, the word "jugo" (juice) is pronounced "hoo-goh."
- When learning Spanish, it's important to consider the pronunciation of "ll" and "y" as they can differ depending on the dialect. However, as a beginner, it may be best to focus on developing a neutral Spanish accent to ensure that you can communicate effectively with Spanish speakers from any country. In neutral Spanish, "ll" and "y" are pronounced the

same way: as a soft "y" sound, similar to the "y" in the English word "yes." For example, the word "pollo," which means chicken, is pronounced "poh-yoh," and "playa" (beach) is pronounced "plah-yah."

5 TIPS TO SOUND MORE NATURAL

Pronunciation is one of the most challenging aspects of learning a new language. But with these **five tips**, you'll be well on your way to sounding more natural in no time:

1. **Focus on one Spanish accent/dialect:** Spanish is spoken in many countries and each country has its own unique accent and dialect. It's important to choose one accent/dialect that you like the most or that you'll be most likely to use in your daily life. For example, if you plan on visiting Mexico, then you should focus on Mexican Spanish. Same with Spain, Chile, and Argentina, since these three are among the most distinctive. This will help you become more comfortable with the sounds and intonations of that particular accent/dialect.
2. **Watch out for Bs and Vs:** In Spanish, the sounds for "B" and "V" are very similar, which can be confusing for non-native speakers. The key to mastering this is to practice, practice, practice! Listen closely to native speakers and try to mimic the way they pronounce these letters. The sound of the letter B is soft:

"bueno" (good); instead, the letter V sounds louder, with a stricter sound, and with a tighter mouth: "valor" (value).

3. **Make an effort to pronounce accents:** Spanish is a language that uses accents to indicate where the emphasis falls in a word. It's important to pay attention to these accents and make an effort to pronounce them correctly. This will make your speech sound more natural and help you avoid misunderstandings.

4. **Practice with tongue twisters:** Tongue twisters are a fun and effective way to practice your pronunciation. They're challenging to say, but with practice, you'll start to master them. Here's an example: "Tres tristes tigres comen trigo en un trigal." The sound made up of a T and an R (tr) is particularly difficult for those who are not familiar with Spanish, so don't get frustrated if you don't make it at the beginning. Give it a shot, and keep trying!

5. **Link words together:** In Spanish, words often sound like they were linked together. It makes it difficult for non-native speakers to understand natives. However, by practicing this technique, you can make your speech sound more natural. For example, instead of saying "yo tengo hambre" (I am hungry), you can link the words together and say "yoten-goham-bre."

With so many resources available online, it can be tempting to rely on online translators to learn new words and phrases. However, while these tools provide an example of how to pronounce words, they don't offer a practical solution for retaining new vocabulary.

That's where a good old-fashioned notebook comes in handy. Writing down each new word and its corresponding phonetic pronunciation in your own phonetic alphabet is a great way to ensure that the new vocabulary stays in your brain. For example, the Spanish word "lluvia" (rain) can sound like "youvia" to an English speaker. Writing it down in your notebook as "lluvia, rain /youvia/" will not only help you remember the word, but it will also aid in your pronunciation. Even better, you can also attach an image of rain so that your brain builds neural bridges and makes the correct associations between images, objects, words, and pronunciation.

Of course, it takes more effort than simply relying on an online translator, but the reward is worth it. By writing down each new word in your notebook, you're actively engaging your brain and committing the new vocabulary to memory. Plus, you'll have a handy reference guide to look back on when you need to recall a word or phrase.

With your trusty notebook in hand, it's time to dive into core vocabulary that will serve as the building blocks for communication. Whether you're learning Spanish for travel, work, or personal enrichment, it's important to start with the basics. From common greetings and expressions to essential verbs and adjectives, the more words you learn, the more confident you'll become in your ability to communicate in Spanish.

If you don't know how to spell it, ask a native speaker to help you with the proper spelling and pronunciation of the word or phrase. This way, you will gradually train your ear to recognize the words and the local speaking style. We Spanish speakers love it when others try to learn our language and we are happy to help them. So, don't be afraid to ask. I promise you that no one will make fun of you!

So, take the time to invest in your language-learning journey. By putting in the effort to write down new vocabulary in your notebook and regularly reviewing it, you'll be on your way to speaking Spanish with ease in no time.

To start incorporating the habit of learning Spanish into your daily life, you can implement some of these simple, fun, and effective didactic tasks. Time to do homework!

- **Make your home a Spanish classroom!** Label everything in your home with its Spanish name. This will help you learn new vocabulary every day without even realizing it. You can start with the kitchen: label the dishes, the cutlery, the utensils, the furniture, etc. The following week you can do the same with the objects in the bedroom, bathroom, and garden, among others.

- **Sing your way to Spanish fluency!** Sing along to Spanish songs and pay attention to the lyrics. This will help you improve your pronunciation and vocabulary. You can opt for slow songs to be able to identify the pronunciations of the words while you hear and read them.
- **Netflix and learn:** Watch Spanish TV shows or movies with English subtitles. Pay attention to how the words sound and try to repeat them out loud.

PRACTICE AND VOCABULARY

1. **Separate the following words into syllables:**
2. Equívoco/a (ambiguous)
3. Análogo/a (analogous)
4. Disuadir (dissuade)
5. Estipulación (stipulation)
6. Evocar (evoke)
7. Frenético/a (frantic)
8. Indolencia (indolence)
9. Influir (influence)
10. Introspección (introspection)
11. Lúdico/a (ludic)
12. Mitigar (mitigate)
13. Paradoja (paradox)
14. Perspicaz (perspicacious)
15. Plausible (plausible)
16. Prejuicio (prejudice)

17. Procrastinar (procrastinate)
18. Propagación (propagation)
19. Recalcitrante (recalcitrant)
20. Resiliente (resilient)
21. Sarcástico/a (sarcastic)
22. Serendipia (serendipity)
23. Sobresaliente (outstanding)
24. Soslayar (bypass)
25. Trascendente (transcendent)
26. Volátil (volatile)

Answers:

1. e-quí-vo-co/a
2. a-ná-lo-go/a
3. di-sua-dir
4. es-ti-pu-la-ción
5. e-vo-car
6. fre-né-ti-co/a
7. in-do-len-cia
8. in-flu-ir
9. in-tros-pec-ción
10. lú-di-co/a
11. mi-ti-gar
12. pa-ra-do-ja
13. pers-pi-caz
14. plau-si-ble
15. pre-jui-cio

16. pro-cras-ti-nar
17. pro-pa-ga-ción
18. re-cal-ci-tran-te
19. re-si-lien-te
20. sar-cás-ti-co/a
21. se-ren-di-pia
22. so-bre-sa-lien-te
23. sos-la-yar
24. tras-cen-den-te
25. vo-lá-til

In Spanish, there are different rules for accentuating a word. The accent or tilde fulfills the function of indicating which is the syllable that is pronounced with more emphasis in a word. Since these rules are a bit complicated and beyond the comprehension of an amateur learner, we are going to skip learning them and instead, I will leave you a list of words with accents in Spanish so that you know them and develop an intuition about them:

- Árbol (tree): ahr-bohl
- Ídolo (idol): ee-doh-loh
- Época (epoch): eh-poh-kah
- Música (music): moo-see-kah
- Fácil (easy): fah-seel
- Útil (useful): oo-teel
- Así (like this, so): ah-see
- Camión (truck): kah-myohn

- Público (public): poo-blee-koh
- Página (page): pah-hee-nah
- Américas (Americas): ah-meh-rih-kahz
- Matemáticas (mathematics): mah-teh-mah-tee-kahs
- Sábado (Saturday): sah-bah-doh
- Único (unique): oo-nee-koh
- Pirámide (pyramid): pee-rah-mee-deh
- Grúa (crane): groo-ah
- Clímax (climax): klee-mahx
- Ejército (army): eh-hehr-see-toh
- Fantástico (fantastic): fahn-tahs-tee-koh
- Esquí (ski): ehs-kee
- Cálido (warm): kah-lee-doh
- Óptimo (optimal): ohp-tee-moh
- Víctima (victim): beek-tee-mah
- Mágico (magical): mah-hee-koh
- Cárcel (jail): kahr-sehl
- Médico (medical): meh-dee-koh
- Ácido (acid): ah-see-doh
- Apólogo (apologue): ah-poh-loh-goh
- Sónico (sonic): soh-nee-koh
- Antártida (Antarctica): ahn-tahr-tee-dah

2

ESSENTIAL SPANISH VOCABULARY

¿Hablas español? Spanish, in particular, is a language with a rich and complex history. From its roots in Latin to the influence of Arabic during the Middle Ages, Spanish has evolved into the magnificent language we know and love today.

The Spanish language is a fascinating and rich language that has an interesting history. The origins of this stunning language can be traced back to the Iberian Peninsula, where the Celtic and Iberian languages were spoken. The Roman Empire conquered the peninsula in the 3rd century BC, and Latin became the language of the land. Over time, Latin evolved into what we now know as Spanish.

Spanish has been greatly influenced by other cultures and languages. In the 8th century AD, the Moors, a Muslim people from North Africa, invaded the peninsula and brought with them the Arabic language. Arabic words can still be found in the Spanish language today. The word "ojala" serves as an example. It has evolved from the Arabic phrase "law šá lláh," which translates to "If god would want it" or "God willing." Today, the word has lost its religious connotation and is primarily used to express "I hope." People of different religions, including Catholics, Christians, Muslims, and atheists, use the word without realizing its origins (WhyNotSpanish, 2018).

As Spain expanded its territories through conquest and colonization in the 15th and 16th centuries, the Spanish language spread throughout the Americas, Africa, and Asia. This led to the emergence of various dialects, each with its own unique characteristics and nuances.

Today, Spanish is the second most spoken language in the world, with over 500 million speakers worldwide. It is the official language of Spain and many Latin American countries, as well as one of the official languages of the United Nations.

The expansion of Spanish has not only contributed to its linguistic influence but has also shaped the culture and identity of the regions where it is spoken. It has been an integral part of the development of literature, art, music, and cinema, and has helped to connect people across borders and cultures (Newsdle, n.d.).

But enough about history, let's get down to business: essential Spanish vocabulary. In this chapter, we will cover a wide range of vocabulary. But we won't just give you a list of words and their translations. We'll also provide you with contextualized examples.

One of the best ways to reinforce new vocabulary is through repetition and practice. That's why I've included exercises and activities to help you master the words you've learned. You'll also have the opportunity to practice your new vocabulary in the context of real-life situations, like ordering food in a restaurant or asking for directions on the street.

By the end of this chapter, you'll have a solid foundation of essential Spanish vocabulary and the confidence to use it in everyday situations. So, grab a pen and paper, and let's get started! ¡Vamos!

Are you ready to dive into the colorful world of Spanish vocabulary? Next, we're going to explore the vibrant and exciting world of colors and shapes. From the deep blue of the ocean to the bright red of a ripe tomato, we'll cover it all!

COLORS, SHAPES, AND SIZES

Here's a quick list of some essential colors in Spanish, their translations to English and their proper Spanish pronunciation:

- rojo (red): rroh-hoh
- azul (blue): ah-sool
- amarillo (yellow): ah-mah-ree-yoh
- naranja (orange): nah-rahng-hah
- verde (green): berh-deh
- morado (purple): moh-rah-doh
- rosado (pink): rrohh-sah-doh
- marrón (brown): mah-rrohn
- negro (black): neh-groh
- blanco (white): blahn-kho
- gris (gray): grees

Now, let's move on to the world of shapes and geometrical figures. I'll also provide you with plenty of opportunities to practice using these words so that they become second nature to you.

- cuadrado (square): kwah-drah-doh
- triángulo (triangle): tree-ahn-goo-loh
- rectángulo (rectangle): rehk-tahn-goo-loh
- círculo (circle): seehr-koo-loh
- elipse (ellipse): eh-leep-seh
- rombo (rhombus): rohm-boh
- trapecio (trapezoid): trah-peh-syoh
- pentágono (pentagon): pehn-tah-goh-noh
- hexágono (hexagon): ehks-ah-goh-noh
- estrella (star): ehs-treh-yah

Now, let's learn about sizes:

- pequeño (little): peh-keh-nyoh
- mediano (medium): meh-dee-ah-noh
- grande (big): grahn-deh

THE HUMAN BODY

Now, let's get started with some basic vocabulary related to the human body. After all, knowing how to describe body parts is not only useful for everyday conversations, but it can also be helpful in emergencies. So, let's start with some translations:

- cabeza (head): kah-beh-sah
- ojos (eyes): oh-hohs
- nariz (nose): nah-reez
- oreja (ear): oh-reh-hah
- boca (mouth): boh-kah
- lengua (tongue): lehn-gwah
- dientes (teeth): dee-ehn-tehs
- labios (lips): lah-bee-ohs
- garganta (throat): gahr-gahn-tah
- cuello (neck): kweh-yoh
- hombro (shoulder): ohm-broh
- espalda (back): ehs-pahl-dah
- pecho (chest): peh-choh
- brazo (arm): brah-soh

- codo (elbow): koh-doh
- mano (hand): mah-noh
- dedo (finger): deh-doh
- cadera (hip): kah-deh-rah
- pierna (leg): pyehr-nah
- rodilla (knee): roh-dee-yah
- tobillo (ankle): toh-bee-yoh
- pie (foot): pyeh
- dedo del pie (toe): deh-doh del pyeh

Now that we have some basic vocabulary, let's explore some fun ways to reinforce it. You can create flashcards with images of each body part and the corresponding word in Spanish. Or, you can practice describing body parts using complete sentences. For example, "Tengo ojos verdes" (I have green eyes) or "Me duele la cabeza" (My head hurts).

CLOTHES AND ACCESSORIES

It's time to talk about "ropa" (clothes) and "accesorios" (accessories). Here's a list of some common vocabulary words to get you started:

- la camisa (the shirt): lah kah-mee-sah
- el pantalón (the pants): el pan-tah-lohn
- la falda (the skirt): lah fahl-dah
- el vestido (the dress): el be-stee-doh
- los zapatos (the shoes): lohs sah-pah-tohs

- las botas (the boots): lahs boh-tahs
- las zapatillas (the sneakers): lahs sah-pah-tee-yahs
- los calcetines (the socks): lohs kahl-seh-tee-nehs
- la corbata (the tie): lah kohr-bah-tah
- el sombrero (the hat): el sohm-breh-roh
- la bufanda (the scarf): lah boo-fahn-dah
- los guantes (the gloves): lohs gwahn-tehs
- las gafas (the glasses): lahs gah-fahs
- el reloj (the watch): el reh-loh
- el bolso (the purse): el bohl-soh

You'll notice that this time I included the articles before the words. This is because, in Spanish, nouns and adjectives have gender, contrary to English where they are gender neutral.

When an object is feminine we say "la" (the), and when it is masculine we use "el" (the). While in English you would say "the car" or "the house," in Spanish you would say "el auto" or "la casa."

Don't worry too much about the gender of the objects we learn for now; this is simply so that your brain can build associations between objects and their gender in Spanish.

Now, here's a fun challenge for you: Look at yourself in the mirror and try to name all the clothes and accessories you're wearing in Spanish. Don't worry if you don't know all the words yet, just give it a try! This is a great way to reinforce your vocabulary and get into the habit of using Spanish in your daily life.

FAMILY AND RELATIONSHIPS

Did you know that family is a very important aspect of Spanish culture? The Spanish language has many words to describe different family members, and it's essential to know them if you want to communicate effectively with native speakers.

So, let's start with the list of family members in Spanish:

- abuela (grandmother): ah-bweh-lah
- abuelo (grandfather): ah-bweh-loh
- madre (mother): mah-dreh
- padre (father): pah-dreh
- hijo/hija (son/daughter): ee-hoh/ee-hah
- hermano/hermana (brother/sister): ehr-mah-noh/ehr-mah-nah
- tío/tía (uncle/aunt): tee-oh/tee-ah
- sobrino/sobrina (nephew/niece): soh-bree-noh/soh-bree-nah
- primo/prima (cousin): pree-moh/pree-mah
- esposo/esposa (husband/wife): ehs-poh-soh/ehs-poh-sah

Now, here comes the fun part! Make a list of the names of your own family members. Do not write the words in English next to each family member, but in Spanish. For example, if you have a sister named Mary, you would write "Hermana: Mary." This way, you will begin to link these concepts with your context.

Remember, it's important to put the vocabulary into context by using your own family members' names. This will help you remember the words more easily and make the learning experience more enjoyable.

AROUND THE HOME

Now, let's move on and learn some useful vocabulary for around the home!

Baño (bathroom): bah-nyoh

- la bañera (the bathtub): lah bahn-yeh-rah
- el inodoro (the toilet): el ee-noh-doh-roh
- el lavabo (the sink): el lah-bah-boh
- la ducha (the shower): lah doo-chah
- la toalla (the towel): lah toh-ah-yah
- el jabón (the soap): el hah-bohn

Sala de estar (living room): sah-lah deh ehs-tahr

- el sofá (the sofa): el soh-fah
- la mesa (the table): lah meh-sah
- la televisión (the television): lah teh-lee-bee-syohn
- la silla (the chair): lah see-yah
- la alfombra (the rug): lah ahl-fohm-brah
- el estante (the bookshelf): el ehs-tahn-teh

- el cuadro (the painting): el kooah-droh

Cocina (kitchen): koh-see-nah

- la estufa (the stove): lah ehs-too-fah
- el refrigerador (the refrigerator): el reh-free-heh-rah-dohr
- el horno (the oven): el ohr-noh
- el fregadero (the sink): el freh-gah-deh-roh
- el plato (the plate): el plah-toh
- el tenedor (the fork): el teh-neh-dohr
- el cuchillo (the knife): el koo-chee-yoh
- la cuchara (the spoon): lah koo-chah-rah
- el vaso (the glass): el bah-soh
- la taza (the cup): lah tah-sah

Cuarto (bedroom): kwahr-toh

- la cama (the bed): lah kah-mah
- las sábanas (the sheets): lahs sah-bah-nahs
- el armario (the closet): el ahr-mah-ryo
- el espejo (the mirror): el ehs-peh-hoh
- la lámpara (the lamp): lah lahmpah-rah
- el reloj despertador (the alarm clock): el reh-loh hdehs-pehr-tah-dohr
- la mesita de noche (the nightstand): lah meh-see-tah deh noh-cheh
- la almohada (the pillow): lah al-moh-ah-dah

Jardín (garden): hahr-deen

- el césped (the lawn): el seh-spehd
- la maceta (the pot): lah mah-seh-tah
- el árbol (the tree): el ahr-bohl
- la flor (the flower): lah flohr
- la manguera (the hose): lah mahn-geh-rah
- la pala (the shovel): lah pah-lah

It's time to put it into practice! I challenge you to (roughly) sketch your own home and label the main parts in Spanish. This will help reinforce the vocabulary you just learned and give you a visual representation of the words. Have fun!

TRAVEL AND TRANSPORT

Are you ready to hit the road and explore beautiful Spanish-speaking countries? Then let's start by learning some essential Spanish vocabulary related to travel and transportation!

Vacaciones (vacations): bah-kah-see-yoh-ness

- el coche/carro/auto (car): el koh-cheh/kah-rroh/ow-toh
- el metro (subway): el meh-troh
- El avión (the plane): ehl ah-vee-ohn
- el aeropuerto (airport): el ah-eh-roh-pwer-toh
- el barco (boat): el bar-koh
- la maleta (suitcase): lah mah-leh-tah

- el billete (ticket): el bee-yeh-teh
- el pasaporte (passport): el pah-sah-pohr-teh
- la carretera (road): lah kah-reh-teh-rah
- la estación (station): lah es-tah-see-yohn
- el equipaje (luggage): el eh-kee-pah-heh

Meet Mary, a travel enthusiast who is going on a holiday to a beautiful island. She will travel by car, metro, and plane to reach her destination.

Mary starts by packing her "maleta" with all the necessary things for her trip, including "ropa," "zapatos," "protector solar," and "gafas de sol." She also makes sure to carry her "billetera" and "pasaporte" with her as they are essential for travel.

Next, she gets into her "coche" and hits the "carretera" towards the city. The road is long and winding, but Mary enjoys the scenic beauty and uses the opportunity to practice her Spanish by singing along to the Spanish radio station.

Once she reaches the city, she parks her car and takes the "metro" to the "aeropuerto." She buys her "billete" and goes through security with her "pasaporte." After some duty-free shopping, she boards the "avión" to the island.

On the "avión," Mary meets some friendly locals and practices her Spanish skills by having a conversation with them. Finally, she reaches the island and collects her "equipaje" before heading to the hotel.

Now, it's your turn! Can you translate all the Spanish vocabulary words Mary used on her journey? Learning new vocabulary is essential for successful travel and a fun way to challenge your brain. So, let's get started and prepare for your next adventure!

Deducing the meaning of words from context is an almost automatic mechanism that leads us to learn a lot when we are exposed to a new language.

JOBS AND THE OFFICE

Enough fun. It's time to talk about work.

Below is a chart with two columns. The first column lists common job titles in Spanish, and the second column is blank for you to try and guess the occupation (many are obvious like "dentista"). But wait! Before you look at the English translations under the chart, try and cover it up and see how many job titles you can guess based on the Spanish word alone.

Spanish Word	Occupation
Cajero	
Abogado	
Cocinero	
Dentista	
Enfermero	
Escritor	
Ingeniero	
Médico	
Periodista	
Programador	
Secretario	
Cajero	
Abogado	
Profesor	

How did you do? Don't worry if you didn't get them all right, that's what we're here to learn! Let's go through the list of jobs in Spanish and their English translations:

- cajero (cashier): kah-heh-roh
- abogado (lawyer): ah-boh-gah-doh
- cocinero (chef): koh-see-neh-roh
- dentista (dentist): den-tee-stah
- enfermero (nurse): ehn-fehr-meh-roh
- escritor (writer): ess-kree-tor
- ingeniero (engineer): een-heh-nee-eh-roh
- médico (doctor): meh-dee-koh
- periodista (journalist): peh-ree-oh-dee-stah
- programador (programmer): proh-grah-mah-dor
- secretario (secretary): seh-kreh-tah-ree-oh
- profesor (teacher): proh-feh-sor
- policia (police officer): poh-lee-see-ah
- vendedor (salesperson): ben-deh-dor
- terapeuta (therapist): teh-rah-pehoo-tah
- dueño de negocios (business owner): doo-eh-nyoh deh neh-goh-see-ohs
- inversionista (investor): een-ver-seeoh-nees-tah
- emprendedor (entrepreneur): em-pren-deh-dor
- deportista (athlete): deh-por-tee-stah
- artista (artist): ar-tees-tah
- científico (scientist): see-en-tee-fee-koh
- político (politician): poh-lee-tee-koh

Now that you have a good base of job titles in Spanish, it's time to reinforce that knowledge. Practice using these words in context by imagining yourself in an office setting or out in the field. You can also try creating flashcards with the

Spanish word on one side and the English translation on the other. And don't forget to use these words in conversation with others who speak Spanish. This may be a little embarrassing for you, but it is a fundamental barrier that you have to face. You can read many manuals to learn Spanish, but you won't learn it if you don't speak it.

SCHOOL SUBJECTS

Learning all these words will not only help you communicate better with Spanish-speaking students and teachers, but it will also broaden your knowledge and understanding of the world.

Here are some of the most common school subjects in Spanish:

- matemáticas (mathematics): mah-teh-mah-tee-kahs
- ciencias (science): see-ehn-see-ahs
- historia (history): ees-toh-ree-ah
- geografía (geography): heh-oh-grah-fee-ah
- lengua y literatura (language and literature): lehn-gwah ee lee-teh-rah-too-rah
- arte (art): ahr-teh
- música (music): moo-see-kah
- educación física (physical education): eh-doo-kah-see-ohn fee-see-kah
- tecnología (technology): tehk-noh-loh-hee-ah
- idiomas (languages): ee-dee-oh-mahs

Try to memorize these words by creating associations with them or making flashcards. Practice saying them out loud and using them in sentences to help you remember them better.

Now that you have learned these new words, it's time to practice! Test yourself by trying to write a sentence using each of these school subjects in Spanish. You can also practice listening and comprehension by watching videos in Spanish about these topics—with English subtitles, of course.

DOMESTIC CHORES

Now, let's talk about household chores! It's not the most glamorous topic, but it's certainly an important one. After all, keeping your living space clean and organized can make a big difference in your overall well-being.

So, let's dive into some vocabulary that will help you tackle those domestic duties with ease. Here are some key verbs to keep in mind:

- limpiar (to clean): leem-pyahr
- desempolvar (to dust): dehs-ehm-pohl-bahr
- barrer (to sweep): bah-rehr
- fregar (to mop): freh-gahr
- aspirar (to vacuum): ah-spee-rahr
- lavar (to wash): lah-bahr

- lavar la ropa (to do the laundry): lah-bahr lah roh-pah
- secar (to dry): seh-kahr
- planchar (to iron): plahn-chahr
- colgar (to hang): kohl-gahr
- recoger (to pick up): reh-koh-hehr
- quitar (to remove): kee-tahr
- sacar la basura (to take out the trash): sah-kahr lah bah-soo-rah
- cortar el césped (to mow): kohr-tahr ehl sehsped
- regar (to water): reh-gahr
- clasificar (to sort): klah-see-fee-kahr

With these verbs in your vocabulary arsenal, you'll be able to describe exactly what needs to be done around the house. Whether it's sweeping up the kitchen (barrer la cocina), vacuuming the living room (aspirar la sala de estar), or doing laundry (lavar ropa), you'll be able to communicate your needs clearly.

ANIMALS

Animals come in all shapes and sizes, and Spanish has a rich vocabulary to describe them all. Let's start with popular pets and farm animals:

- perro (dog): peh-roh
- gato (cat): gah-toh

- conejo (rabbit): koh-neh-hoh
- pájaro (bird): pah-hah-roh
- caballo (horse): kah-bah-yoh
- vaca (cow): bah-kah
- cerdo (pig): sehr-doh
- oveja (sheep): oh-veh-hah
- gallina (chicken): gah-yee-nah
- pato (duck): pah-toh

Moving on to land animals:

- león (lion): leh-ohn
- tigre (tiger): tee-greh
- mono (monkey): moh-noh
- elefante (elephant): eh-leh-fahn-teh
- jirafa (giraffe): hee-rah-fah
- zorro (fox): soh-roh
- oso (bear): oh-soh
- lobo (wolf): loh-boh
- cebra (zebra): seh-brah
- rinoceronte (rhinoceros): ree-noh-seh-rohn-teh

And lastly, aquatic animals:

- tiburón (shark): tee-boo-rohn
- ballena (whale): bah-yeh-nah
- delfín (dolphin): dehl-feen
- pulpo (octopus): pool-poh

- caballito de mar (seahorse): kah-bah-yee-toh deh mahr
- pez (fish): pehz
- cangrejo (crab): kahn-greh-hoh
- langosta (lobster): lahng-goh-stah
- medusa (jellyfish): meh-doo-sah
- estrella de mar (starfish): ehs-treh-yah deh mahr

HOBBIES

Now that we have explored the world of animals, let's shift gears and delve into the realm of personal interests and hobbies. Just as the animal kingdom boasts a remarkable array of species, humans, too, exhibit a vast range of passions and activities that captivate their hearts and minds. So, let's learn some of the most common hobbies and interests in Spanish:

- bailar (to dance): bah-ee-lahr
- cocinar (to cook): koh-see-nahr
- leer (to read): leh-ehr
- ver películas (to watch movies): behr peh-lee-koo-lahs
- escuchar música (to listen to music): ehs-koo-char moo-see-kah
- jugar videojuegos (to play video games): hoo-gahr bee-deh-oh-hweh-gohs
- hacer deporte (to do sports): ah-sehr deh-pohr-teh

- pintar (to paint): peen-tahr
- viajar (to travel): bee-ah-hahr
- escribir (to write): ehs-kree-beer

To practice talking about your hobbies, try using the phrase "Me gusta (meh goos-tah)" which means "I like." For example, "Me gusta bailar (meh goos-tah bahy-lahr)" means "I like dancing." You can also use "No me gusta (noh meh goos-tah)," which means "I don't like."

You now have a diverse range of vocabulary under your belt. By learning about animals, jobs, and hobbies, you've opened up a world of possibilities in your Spanish-speaking journey. From discussing your pets and favorite animals to talking about your job and hobbies, you'll have plenty to say in conversations with native Spanish speakers. But don't stop here! In the next chapter, we'll dive deeper into time expressions, so you can add more context and meaning to your newfound vocabulary. Keep up the good work!

PRACTICE AND VOCABULARY

1. **Label everything!** You can label different elements according to their color and shape. You can also stick a list on the door of your closet with the name of each item of clothing and, just in case, a drawing or two.

2. **Play the role**: Your family and pets may not like that you label them so instead try to always refer to them with the word in Spanish. For example, you can have your mom on your cell phone as "mamá" instead of "mom."
3. **Practice "I like" and "I don't like":** You can build many sentences from what you know so far. List the animals, clothes, things, and jobs you like, as well as those you don't. For example: "I like the lion" or "I don't like to work."
4. **Read the text and answer the questions below. Try not to check the translation unless is necessary.**

Lola es una niña pequeña. Ella tiene una bufanda roja y unas zapatillas amarillas. Hoy se siente aventurera y decide salir al parque. Allí ve muchas cosas de colores diferentes, como una flor naranja, un elefante gris, un cangrejo rojo y una estrella de mar morada. También ve a un deportista corriendo y a un policía patrullando en su coche.

Luego de jugar un rato, Lola regresa a casa y ayuda a su abuela a fregar los platos y a sacar la basura. Después de lavar sus manos, Lola se sienta en el sofá y lee una historia sobre un conejo que vive en el bosque. Mientras lee, se rasca la espalda. Está molesta porque le duele un poco la rodilla y el pie. Finalmente, Lola se queda dormida.

Translation:

Lola is a little girl. She has a red scarf and yellow sneakers. Today, she feels adventurous and decides to go out to the park. There she sees many things of different colors, such as an orange flower, a gray elephant, a red crab, and a purple starfish. She also sees a jogging athlete and a patrolling police officer in her car.

After playing for a while, Lola returns home and helps her grandmother wash the dishes and take out the trash. After washing her hands, Lola sits on the sofa and reads a story about a rabbit that lives in the forest. As she reads, she scratches her back. She is upset because her knee and foot hurt a little. Finally, Lola falls asleep.

Questions:

1. ¿Cómo se llama la niña de la historia?
2. ¿De qué color es la bufanda de Lola?
3. ¿Qué animal de color rojo ve Lola en el parque?
4. ¿Qué hace Lola cuando regresa a casa?
5. ¿Por qué está molesta Lola mientras lee la historia?

Answers:

1. Lola. (Lola.)
2. Roja. (Red.)
3. Un cangrejo. (A crab.)

4. Ayuda a su abuela a fregar los platos y a sacar la basura. (She helps her grandmother wash the dishes and take out the garbage.)
5. Porque le duele un poco la rodilla y el pie. (Because her knee and foot hurt a little.)

3

NUMBERS AND TIME

In this chapter, we will cover the essentials of numbers and time in Spanish. We'll start with the basics, such as cardinal and ordinal numbers, and progress to more complex expressions like dates and telling time, and talking about the weather.

Along the way, I'll provide useful tips and tricks to make sure you're confident in using these expressions in real-life situations. By the end of this chapter, you'll be able to express dates and times accurately and avoid any embarrassing or costly misunderstandings. So, let's dive in and get started with the world of Spanish numbers and time!

CARDINAL AND ORDINAL NUMBERS

Let's start with cardinal numbers, which are used to count things or people.

Here are the first 20 cardinal numbers:

0. cero (ceh-roh)
1. uno (oo-noh)
2. dos (dohs)
3. tres (trehs)
4. cuatro (kwat-roh)
5. cinco (seen-koh)
6. seis (sayss)
7. siete (syeh-teh)
8. ocho (oh-choh)
9. nueve (nweh-veh)
10. diez (dyehs)
11. once (ohn-seh)
12. doce (doh-seh)
13. trece (treh-seh)
14. catorce (kah-tor-seh)
15. quince (keen-seh)
16. dieciséis (dyeh-see-sees)
17. diecisiete (dyeh-see-syeh-teh)
18. dieciocho (dyeh-see-oh-choh)
19. diecinueve (dyeh-see-nweh-veh)
20. veinte (beyn-teh)

In Spanish, numbers are composed by using the same system as in English with the exception of the numbers 11 through 15. In English, these numbers are composed of a "teen" suffix (thirteen, fourteen, fifteen), but in Spanish, they are formed by adding the suffix -ce to the corresponding root number. For example, eleven in Spanish is "once" (1 + 10), and twelve is "doce" (2 + 10).

After 15, the root number is used followed by the conjunction "y" (and) and the corresponding unit number. For example, 16 is "dieciséis" (10 + 6), 17 is "diecisiete" (10 + 7), and so on.

Here you have some examples of numbers above 20:

- 24: veinticuatro (vayn-tee-kwah-troh)
- 31: treinta y uno (trayn-tah ee oo-noh)
- 46: cuarenta y seis (kwar-en-tah ee seis)
- 58: cincuenta y ocho (seen-kwen-tah ee oh-choh)
- 60: sesenta (seh-sehn-tah)
- 79: setenta y nueve (seh-ten-tah ee noo-eh-veh)
- 82: ochenta y dos (oh-chen-tah ee dohs)
- 95: noventa y cinco (noh-ven-tah ee seen-koh)
- 100: cien (syehn)
- 120: ciento veinte (see-ehn-toh vayn-teh)

Additionally, when expressing numbers in Spanish, it's common to use a period instead of a comma to separate the decimal and whole numbers. For example, the number 3.14

in Spanish would be written as 3,14, since the dot is used to separate magnitude orders—in Spanish, you would write 1.000.000 for a million, while in English you would write 1,000,000. In short, where dots are used in English, commas are used in Spanish and vice versa.

Here you have some examples to see it more clearly:

- 2.5 (English) - 2,5 (Spanish)
- 3,567.89 (English) - 3.567,89 (Spanish)
- 12,345,678 (English) - 12.345.678 (Spanish)
- 0.75 (English) - 0,75 (Spanish)

Now, let's move on to the ordinal numbers, which are used to indicate the position of something in a series. Here are the first 10 ordinal numbers:

1. primero (pree-meh-roh): first
2. segundo (seh-goon-doh): second
3. tercero (tehr-seh-roh): third
4. cuarto (kwar-toh): fourth
5. quinto (keen-toh): fifth
6. sexto (seks-toh): sixth
7. séptimo (sep-tee-moh): seventh
8. octavo (ohk-tah-voh): eighth
9. noveno (noh-beh-noh): ninth
10. décimo (deh-see-moh): tenth

Knowing how to say numbers up to the thousands can also come in handy.

Here's a brief guide on how to say larger numbers in Spanish:

- 1.000: mil (meel)
- 10.000: diez mil (dyehss meel)
- 100.000: cien mil (syehn meel)
- 1.000.000: un millón (oon mee-yohn)

TELLING THE TIME

When it comes to telling time, the 24-hour clock is commonly used in Spain. So, for example, 3:00 pm would be expressed as "15:00." However, it's also common to use the 12-hour clock in everyday conversation. To say "in the morning" or "in the afternoon/evening," use the phrases "de la mañana" or "de la tarde/noche," respectively.

As we all know, time is of the essence, and mastering this skill will help you avoid unnecessary confusion and embarrassment.

Let's start with the basics, shall we? To say "It's 1 o'clock" in Spanish, you simply say "Es la una." Easy peasy, right? But after that, things get a little trickier.

For all the other hours, you'll need to use "son las" followed by the number. For example, "Son las dos" means "It's 2 o'clock." And if you want to say "It's half past 2," you would say "Son las dos y media."

Moving on to the minutes, you can use the phrase "y" to indicate "and." For example, "Son las tres y quince" means "It's 3:15." You can also use the phrase "menos" to indicate "minus." So "Son las cuatro menos veinte" means "It's 3:40."

It may seem daunting at first, but with practice, you'll soon be telling time like a pro! To help you on your journey, here are some examples of how to tell the time in Spanish:

- Es la una (es lah oo-nah): It's one o'clock
- Son las dos (sohn lahs dohs): It's two o'clock
- Son las tres y cuarto (sohn lahs trayz ee kwahr-toh): It's quarter past three
- Son las cuatro y media (sohn lahs kwah-troh ee mah-dee-ah): It's half past four
- Son las cinco y cuarenta y cinco (sohn lahs seen-koh ee kwah-rehn-tah ee seen-koh): It's five forty-five.
- Son las seis en punto (sohn lahs sayz ehn poon-toh): It's six o'clock sharp
- Son las siete y diez (sohn lahs syeh-teh ee dyehs): It's ten past seven
- Son las ocho y veinte (sohn lahs oh-choh ee beyn-teh): It's twenty past eight
- Son las nueve y media (sohn lahs nweh-veh ee meh-dyah): It's half past nine

- Son las diez menos veinticinco (sohn lahs dyehs meh-nohs beyn-tee-seen-koh): It's twenty-five to ten

DAYS, MONTHS, AND SEASONS

Now, it's time to cover days, months, and seasons.

Let's start with the days of the week:

- Lunes (loo-nehs): Monday
- Martes (mahr-tehs): Tuesday
- Miércoles (mee-ehr-koh-lehs): Wednesday
- Jueves (hweh-behs): Thursday
- Viernes (bee-ehr-nehs): Friday
- Sábado (sah-bah-doh): Saturday
- Domingo (doh-meen-goh): Sunday

Now, let's move on to the months of the year:

- Enero (eh-neh-roh): January
- Febrero (feh-breh-roh): February
- Marzo (mahr-soh): March
- Abril (ah-breehl): April
- Mayo (mah-yoh): May
- Junio (hoo-nee-oh): June
- Julio (hoo-lee-oh): July
- Agosto (ah-goh-stoh): August
- Septiembre (sehp-tee-yehm-breh): September
- Octubre (ohk-too-breh): October

- Noviembre (noh-byehm-breh): November
- Diciembre (dee-see-yehm-breh): December

It's also important to know the seasons in Spanish:

- Primavera (pree-mah-veh-rah): Spring
- Verano (beh-rah-noh): Summer
- Otoño (oh-toh-nyoh): Fall
- Invierno (een-vyehr-noh): Winter

When discussing a date, it's essential to note that Spanish uses cardinal numbers rather than ordinal numbers, which are used in English. For example, in English, we say "March 15th," while in Spanish, it is "15 de marzo." Additionally, years in Spanish are said as complete numbers. For example, the year 2023 is "dos mil veintitrés," unlike English, where you would split the year into two parts (twenty-twenty-three for 2023).

TALKING ABOUT THE WEATHER

When it comes to discussing the weather in Spanish, it's important to know how to express the temperature, as well as other conditions like rain, snow, wind, and humidity. Here are some common weather expressions in Spanish:

- Está frío (eh-stah free-oh): It's cold.
- Está caluroso (eh-stah kah-loo-rho-soh): It's hot.

- Está nevado (eh-stah neh-vah-doh): It's snowy.
- Está lluvioso (eh-stah yoo-vee-oh-soh): It's rainy.
- Está ventoso (eh-stah ben-toh-soh): It's windy.
- Está húmedo (eh-stah oo-meh-doh): It's humid.

It's important to note that these expressions use the verb "estar" (to be) instead of "ser" (to be) because weather conditions are temporary and subject to change.

When describing temperature, you will have to use the Celsius scale, since all Spanish-speaking countries use the International Metric System units. In Spanish, Celsius is usually used, and it's expressed as "grados Celsius" or just "grados" for short.

For example:

- Hace veinte grados Celsius: It's 20 degrees Celsius. (ah-seh beyn-teh grah-dohs sehl-see-yoos)
- Hace treinta y dos grados: It's 32 degrees. (ah-seh trehn-tah ee dohs grah-dohs)

By learning these expressions, you'll be able to discuss the weather and make small talk with others. Plus, you'll be able to understand weather forecasts and plan your activities accordingly.

ADVERBS OF TIME

Adverbs of time are essential in Spanish to express when an action occurred or how frequently it happens. Here is a list of some common adverbs of time that you can use in your everyday conversations:

- ahora (ah-oh-rah): now
- antes (ahn-tes): before
- después (dehs-pwehs): after
- pronto (prohn-toh): soon
- tarde (tar-deh): late
- temprano (tem-pran-oh): early
- nunca (noon-kah): never
- siempre (see-ehm-preh): always

Additionally, here are some time expressions that can be helpful to communicate more specific points in time:

- hoy (oi): today
- ayer (ah-yehr): yesterday
- mañana (mah-nyah-nah): tomorrow
- la semana pasada (lah se-man-ah pah-sa-dah): last week
- el mes pasado (el mes pah-sa-doh): last month
- el año pasado (el ahn-yo pah-sa-doh): last year
- la próxima semana (lah proh-ksih-mah se-man-ah): next week

- el próximo mes (el proh-ksih-moh mes): next month
- el próximo año (el proh-ksih-moh ahn-yo): next year
- mañana (mah-nyah-nah): morning
- mediodía (meh-dee-oh-dee-ah): noon
- tarde (tahr-deh): afternoon
- noche (noh-cheh): night
- madrugada (mah-droo-gah-dah): early morning/dawn

With these adverbs and expressions of time, you'll be able to confidently communicate when certain things happen and for how long.

PRACTICE AND VOCABULARY

1. In order to help you practice your skills in using numbers and time expressions, I have prepared a list of 25 phrases for you to translate. Make sure to write your translations to Spanish in the space provided after the phrase:

    A. 5:25 am on Monday:_____
    B. Monday the 16th of June:_____
    C. May 1853:_____
    D. The day before yesterday:_____
    E. 3:45 pm:_____
    F. September 12th, 2005:_____
    G. In two weeks:_____

H. Quarter past nine:_____
I. Next Thursday at 8 am:_____
J. December 31st, 1999:_____
K. Five minutes to eleven:_____
L. 13:50 hours:_____
M. Friday the 13th:_____
N. Last Friday:_____
O. August 1st, 2022:_____
P. 11:11 pm:_____
Q. Second Monday in January:_____
R. Three days ago:_____
S. October 23rd, 1976:_____
T. Half past six:_____
U. At noon:_____
V. First week of the month:_____
W. At early morning:_____
X. April 15th, 2024:_____
Y. Half past nine in the evening:_____

Answers:

A. 5:25 de la madrugada del lunes

B. Lunes 16 de junio

C. Mayo de 1853

D. Anteayer

E. 3:45 de la tarde

F. 12 de septiembre de 2005

G. En dos semanas

H. Las nueve y cuarto
I. El próximo jueves a las 8 de la mañana
J. 31 de diciembre de 1999
K. Faltan cinco minutos para las once
L. 13:50 horas
M. Viernes 13
N. El viernes pasado
O. 1 de agosto de 2022
P. 11:11 de la noche
Q. Segundo lunes de enero
R. Hace tres días
S. 23 de octubre de 1976
T. Las seis y media
U. Al mediodía
V. La primera semana del mes
W. A primera hora de la mañana
X. 15 de abril de 2024
Y. Las nueve y media de la noche

2. Read and answer:

Es un día caluroso de verano en septiembre. Son las tres y cuarto de la tarde y hace treinta y dos grados. En este momento, estoy sentado en la oficina, tratando de concentrarme en mi trabajo. Ayer fue un día muy ocupado, pero hoy parece que será un poco más tranquilo.

El próximo mes, estaré de vacaciones. Me iré a una

playa hermosa en México y estoy muy emocionado. Esta noche, voy a hacer planes para mi viaje y pensar en todo lo que quiero hacer. Primero, quiero disfrutar de la playa y el mar. Segundo, quiero visitar algunas ruinas antiguas. Y tercero, quiero probar la comida local. Me encanta la comida mexicana. Creo que diez mil pesos serán suficientes para cubrir todos mis gastos durante el viaje.

Translation:

It is a hot summer day in September. It's a quarter past three in the afternoon and it's thirty-two degrees. Right now, I'm sitting in the office, trying to focus on my work. Yesterday was a very busy day, but today it looks like it will be a bit calmer.
Next month, I'll be on vacation. I'm going to a beautiful beach in Mexico and I'm very excited. Tonight, I'm going to make plans for my trip and think about everything I want to do. First, I want to enjoy the beach and the sea. Second, I want to visit some ancient ruins. And third, I want to try the local food. I love Mexican food. I think that ten thousand pesos will be enough to cover all my expenses during the trip.

Questions:

1. ¿En qué mes está ambientada la historia?
2. ¿Dónde irá de vacaciones el narrador?
3. ¿Qué quiere hacer el narrador durante su viaje?
4. ¿Cuánto dinero piensa que será suficiente para su viaje?

Answers:

1. La historia está ambientada en septiembre. (The story is set in September.)
2. El narrador irá de vacaciones a una playa hermosa en México. (The narrator will go on vacation to a beautiful beach in Mexico.)
3. El narrador quiere disfrutar de la playa y el mar, visitar algunas ruinas antiguas y probar la comida local. (The narrator wants to enjoy the beach and sea, visit some ancient ruins, and try the local food.)
4. El narrador piensa que diez mil pesos serán suficientes para cubrir todos sus gastos durante el viaje. (The narrator thinks that ten thousand pesos will be enough to cover all his expenses during the trip.)

Don't worry if you find some of these phrases challenging at first. Remember to take your time and use your knowledge of the vocabulary and grammar that we've covered in this chapter. With a little practice, you'll be able to recognize dates and times easily and use them effectively in your everyday communication.

You can use this list as a reference tool as you continue to develop your language skills. Good luck!

4

COMMON WORDS AND PHRASES FOR EVERYDAY SITUATIONS

Welcome to Chapter 4 of our Spanish language learning journey! By this point, you've learned essential vocabulary and gained some insights into the rich history of the language. Now, it's time to focus on everyday conversations and build your confidence in speaking Spanish.

In this chapter, we'll be covering common words and phrases that you can use in a wide range of situations. But more than that, I'll also give you the tools to maintain and deepen your conversations by asking questions and exploring topics in more detail.

Meet Sarah, a curious and open-minded traveler who has always been fascinated by Spanish culture. She was on a backpacking trip through Spain and stumbled upon a small village that piqued her interest. As she explored the village, she noticed something peculiar: the locals seemed to greet each other with various greetings, but there didn't seem to be any particular rule on when to use which one.

She would hear "Hola" or "Buenos días" in the morning, "Adiós" or "Hasta luego" in the evening, and "Hasta mañana" or "Hasta pronto" throughout the day. Sarah found this confusing, and she couldn't help but wonder if she was doing something wrong by not following the proper protocol.

To make matters worse, she discovered that the rules for time were also different from what she was used to. In English, it's customary to say "Good morning" until noon, "Good afternoon" from noon until evening, and "Good evening" from evening until night. However, in this village, people would say "Buenas tardes" (good afternoon) after they had eaten lunch, which could be as early as 11:30 am.

This only added to Sarah's confusion, as she struggled to adapt to the unfamiliar cultural norms. She would often find herself second-guessing which greeting to use or when to use it. Despite this, Sarah appreciated the warm and welcoming nature of the locals and continued to explore the village with an open mind, eager to learn more about their unique way of life.

If you are like Sarah, you're probably a little confused too about the different greetings that Spanish speakers use, but don't worry! By the end of this chapter, you'll have a good grasp on these cultural nuances and the confidence to navigate everyday conversations with ease, as Sarah did.

FIRST IMPRESSIONS

Here you have a list with useful examples for diverse situations:

Saludos (Greetings):

- ¡Hola! (oh-lah): Hello!
- ¡Buenos días! (bweh-nohs dee-as): Good morning!
- ¡Buenas tardes! (bweh-nahs tar-des): Good afternoon!
- ¡Buenas noches! (bweh-nahs noh-ches): Good evening/night!
- ¡Hola, qué tal? (oh-lah, keh tal): Hi, how are you?
- ¿Cómo estás? (koh-moh ehs-tahs): How are you?
- ¿Qué pasa? (keh pah-sah): What's up?
- ¡Encantado/a! (en-kahn-tah-doh/dah): Nice to meet you!
- ¡Mucho gusto! (moo-choh goos-toh): Nice to meet you!
- ¡Bienvenido/a! (bee-en-veh-nee-doh/dah): Welcome!
- ¡Saludos! (sah-lu-dohs): Greetings!

Presentaciones (Introductions):

- Me llamo [name]. (meh yah-moh): My name is [name].
- Soy de [place]. (soy deh): I'm from [place].
- ¿Y tú? (ee too): And you?
- Él/Ella es [name]. (el/eh-yah es): He/She is [name].
- Éstos son mis amigos. (ehs-tohs sohn mees ah-mee-gohs): These are my friends.
- Permíteme presentarte a... (pehr-mee-teh-meh prehsen-tar-teh ah): Allow me to introduce you to...

Despedidas (Farewells):

- ¡Adiós! (ah-dee-ohs): Goodbye!
- ¡Hasta luego! (ahs-tah loo-eh-goh): See you later!
- ¡Hasta pronto! (ahs-tah prohn-toh): See you soon!
- ¡Nos vemos! (nohs veh-mohs): See you!
- ¡Chao! (chow): Bye!
- ¡Que tengas un buen día! (keh tehn-gahs un bwehn dee-ah): Have a nice day!
- ¡Que descanses! (keh dehs-kahn-sehs: Rest well!
- ¡Hasta la próxima! (ahs-tah lah proks-ee-mah): Until next time!

Saludos de festividades (Holiday Greetings):

- ¡Feliz Navidad! (feh-lees nah-vee-dahd): Merry Christmas!
- ¡Feliz Año Nuevo! (feh-lees ahn-yoh new-eh-voh): Happy New Year!
- ¡Felices Fiestas! (feh-lee-sehs fyehs-tahs): Happy Holidays!
- ¡Feliz Día de Acción de Gracias! (feh-lees dee-ah deh ahk-see-on deh grah-see-ahs): Happy Thanksgiving!
- ¡Feliz Día de San Valentín! (feh-lees dee-ah deh sahn bah-lehn-teen): Happy Valentine's Day!
- ¡Felíz día de los Muertos! (feh-lees dee-ah deh lohs mwehr-tohs): Happy Day of the Dead!
- ¡Feliz Día de la Madre! (feh-lees dee-ah deh lah mah-dreh): Happy Mother's Day!
- ¡Feliz Día del Padre! (feh-lees dee-ah del pah-dreh): Happy Father's Day!
- ¡Feliz cumpleaños! (feh-lees koom-ple-ah-nyohs): Happy Birthday!

Have you ever been in a conversation with someone and wanted to ask a question but didn't know how? Or maybe you were asked a question in Spanish but had no idea what was being asked? Now, we will cover the eight question words in Spanish and how to use them. Plus, we will also explore how to ask and answer both closed and open-ended questions. By the end, you'll be able to confidently participate in any conversation!

ASKING AND ANSWERING QUESTIONS

First, let's take a look at the eight question words in Spanish:

- ¿Quién? (khi-ehn): Who?
- ¿Qué? (keh): What?
- ¿Cuál? (kwahl): Which?
- ¿Dónde? (dohn-deh): Where?
- ¿Cuándo? (kwahn-doh): When?
- ¿Por qué? (pohr-keh): Why?
- ¿Cómo? (koh-moh): How?
- ¿Cuánto/a? (kwahn-toh/ah): How much/many?

Remember to pay attention to the accents on question words. Without an accent, it's a relative pronoun. And in written Spanish, there is an upside-down question mark at the beginning of the sentence. This is because there are no auxiliary verbs to indicate that the sentence is a question. In Spanish, you write a question the same as a statement. Except for the accent marks, question marks, and the tonality with which the phrase is said, both are indistinguishable. That is why it is important to pay attention to these details. For example, the question "¿Hoy está frío?" (Is it cold today?) is very similar to the statement "Hoy está frío" (Today is cold).

Closed questions are those that require a yes or no answer. Here are some examples:

- ¿Eres de España? (eh-res deh eh-span-ya): Are you from Spain?
- ¿Hablas español? (ah-blahs eh-spah-nyol): Do you speak Spanish?
- ¿Te gusta la música? (teh goos-ta lah moo-see-kah): Do you like music?
- ¿Has viajado al extranjero? (ahs bee-ah-hah-doh ahl ex-trahn-heh-roh): Have you traveled abroad?
- ¿Estás cansado/a? (ehs-tahs kan-sah-doh/kan-sah-dah): Are you tired?
- ¿Tienes hermanos? (tee-eh-nehs ehr-mah-nohs): Do you have siblings?

Open-ended questions require a more detailed response and cannot be answered with a simple yes or no. Here are some examples:

- ¿Quién eres? (khi-ehn eh-rehs): Who are you?
- ¿Cuándo es tu cumpleaños? (kwan-doh ehs too koom-pleh-ahn-yohs): When is your birthday?
- ¿De dónde eres? (deh dohn-deh eh-rehs): Where are you from?
- ¿Qué tiempo hace hoy? (keh tee-ehm-poh ah-seh oh-ee): What's the weather like today?
- ¿Qué hora es? (keh oh-rah ehs): What time is it?

- ¿Cómo te llamas? (koh-moh teh yah-mahs): What's your name?
- ¿Qué estás haciendo? (keh ehs-tahs ah-see-ehn-doh): What are you doing?
- ¿Cuántos años tienes? (kwahn-tohs ahn-yohs tee-eh-nehs): How old are you?
- ¿Dónde vives? (dohn-deh vee-vehs): Where do you live?
- ¿Qué te gusta hacer en tu tiempo libre? (keh teh goos-ta ah-sehr ehn too tee-ehm-poh lee-breh): What do you like to do in your free time?
- ¿Qué tipo de música te gusta? (keh tee-poh deh moo-see-kah teh goos-ta): What kind of music do you like?
- ¿A qué hora te despiertas normalmente? (ah keh oh-rah teh dehs-pyehr-tahs nohr-mahl-mehn-teh): What time do you usually wake up?

ORDERING FOOD AND DRINKS

Food plays a vital role in the cultures of Spanish-speaking countries, where culinary traditions have been shaped by a rich history and diverse geography. From the spicy flavors of Mexico to the delicate seafood dishes of Spain, each country offers a unique gastronomic experience that is not to be missed. Whether you are exploring the bustling streets of Buenos Aires or the charming plazas of Lima, trying the local cuisine is a must-do activity that will allow you to fully immerse yourself in the culture. To help you navigate the menus and order like a local, here are some common phrases and vocabulary words that you can use when dining at a restaurant:

- ¿Nos puede dar la carta, por favor? (nohs pweh-deh dar lah kahr-tah, pohr fah-bor): Can you give us the menu, please?
- Queremos pedir ahora. (keh-reh-mohs peh-deer aho-rah): We want to order now.
- ¿Cuál es la especialidad de la casa? (kwahl ehs lah ess-peh-see-ahl-ee-dahd deh lah kah-sah): What is the specialty of the house?
- ¿Cuál es la sopa del día? (kwahl ehs lah soh-pah del dee-ah): What is the soup of the day?
- ¿Qué recomienda? (keh reh-koh-mee-ehn-dah): What do you recommend?
- ¿Qué lleva este plato? (keh yeh-bah eh-steh plah-toh): What does this dish have?
- ¿Hay algo sin gluten? (ay ahl-goh seen gloo-ten): Is there anything gluten-free?
- La cuenta, por favor. (lah kwehn-tah, pohr fah-bor): The bill, please.

Here you'll find some useful vocabulary:

- El menú (ehl meh-noo): The menu
- La carta (lah kahr-tah): The menu
- La comida (lah koh-mee-dah): The food
- El plato (ehl plah-toh): The dish
- La sopa (lah soh-pah): The soup
- El arroz (ehl ah-rrohz): The rice
- El pollo (ehl poh-yoh): The chicken
- El pescado (ehl peh-skah-doh): The fish
- El postre (ehl pohs-treh): The dessert
- La cuenta (lah kwehn-tah): The bill

Remember to use "por favor" (please) and "gracias" (thank you) when speaking with the waiter or waitress. Buen provecho! (Enjoy your meal!)

Food and drink vocabulary:

Especias/Condimentos	Spices/Seasonings
Sal	Salt
Pimienta	Pepper
Comino	Cumin
Orégano	Oregano
Tomillo	Thyme
Canela	Cinnamon
Clavo de olor	Clove
Verduras	**Vegetables**
Ajo	Garlic
Cebolla	Onion
Lechuga	Lettuce
Tomate	Tomato
Espinaca	Spinach
Zanahoria	Carrot

Pimiento	Bell pepper
Calabacín/Zapallito	Zucchini
Maiz	Corn
Frutas	**Fruits**
Fresa	Strawberry
Kiwi	Kiwi
Piña	Pineapple
Manzana	Apple
Naranja	Orange
Uva	Grape
Plátano/Banana	Banana
Limón	Lemon
Aguacate	Avocado
Pan	**Bread**
Harina	Flour
Avena	Oats
Cebada	Barley
Granos	**Grains**
Arroz	Rice
Quinoa	Quinoa

Carnes	**Meats**
Carne de res	Beef
Cerdo	Pork
Mariscos	Seafood
Bebidas	**Drinks**
Agua	Water
Té	Tea
Café	Coffee
Refresco/Gaseosa	Soft drink/Soda
Cerveza	Beer
Vino	Wine

Here's a chart with some famous meals from different Spanish-speaking countries and their ingredients:

Dish	Country	Ingredients
Paella	Spain	Arroz (rice), pollo (chicken), conejo (rabbit), mariscos (seafood), pimiento (bell pepper), cebolla (onion), ajo (garlic), tomate (tomato), azafrán (saffron), aceite de oliva (olive oil)
Empanadas	Argentina	Carne (beef), cebolla (onion), pimiento (bell pepper), aceitunas (olives), huevo (egg), aceite (oil), harina (flour), sal (salt)
Ceviche	Peru	Pescado (fish), cebolla (onion), ají (chili), limón (lime), cilantro (coriander), choclo (corn), camote (sweet potato)
Tacos al pastor	Mexico	Carne de cerdo (pork), piña (pineapple), cebolla (onion), cilantro (coriander), limón (lime), tortillas de maíz (corn tortillas)
Gallo pinto	Costa Rica	Arroz (rice), frijoles (beans), cebolla (onion), pimiento (bell pepper), ajo (garlic), cilantro (coriander), sal (salt)
Lomo saltado	Peru	Carne de res (beef), cebolla (onion), tomate (tomato), ajo (garlic), pimiento (bell pepper), papas fritas (French fries), arroz (rice), salsa de soja (soy sauce)
Pabellón criollo	Venezuela	Carne mechada (shredded beef), arroz (rice), frijoles negros (black beans), plátano maduro (ripe plantain), queso blanco (white cheese)

Dish	Country	Ingredients
Arroz con pollo	Puerto Rico	Arroz (rice), pollo (chicken), sofrito (sauce made with onion, garlic, bell pepper, cilantro), ajo (garlic), guisantes (peas), pimiento (bell pepper), caldo de pollo (chicken broth)
Asado	Argentina	Carne de vaca (beef), chorizo (sausage), morcilla (blood sausage), chinchulines (chitterlings), mollejas (sweetbreads), ensalada (salad)

MAKING RESERVATIONS AND APPOINTMENTS

Making reservations and appointments can be a nerve-racking experience when you're trying to do it in a foreign language. But with a little bit of practice and the right vocabulary, you'll be able to schedule meetings, appointments, and reservations with comfort in Spanish.

Here are some essential vocabulary words and phrases to help you navigate through the process:

- Reservar (reh-ser-vahr): to reserve
- Hacer una cita (ah-sehr oo-nah see-tah): to make an appointment
- Confirmar (kohn-feer-mahr): to confirm
- Cancelar (kahn-seh-lahr): to cancel
- Disculpar (dees-kool-pahr): to apologize

When making appointments or reservations, it's important to be clear and concise. Here are some useful phrases to keep in mind:

- ¿Podría reservar una mesa para dos, por favor? (Could I reserve a table for two, please?)
- Quisiera hacer una cita con el doctor. (I would like to make an appointment with the doctor.)
- ¿Podría confirmar mi reserva? (Could you confirm my reservation?)
- Lamentablemente, tengo que cancelar mi cita. (Unfortunately, I have to cancel my appointment.)
- Le pido disculpas por cualquier inconveniente que esto pueda causar. (I apologize for any inconvenience this may cause.)

If you're making appointments or reservations for a business meeting or event, it's important to use formal language. Here are some phrases to help you sound professional:

- Me comunico con usted en relación a... (I am contacting you in regards to...)
- Por medio de la presente, quisiera solicitar una cita con... (I would like to request an appointment with...)
- Por favor, háganme saber si esto es posible. (Please let me know if this is possible.)
- Agradezco de antemano su atención. (I appreciate your attention in advance.)

MONEY MATTERS

It's time to move on to practical vocabulary that can help you navigate your day-to-day life, specifically when it comes to money. Here are some important money-related words and phrases in Spanish that you should know:

- Dinero (dee-neh-roh): Money
- Billete (bee-yeh-teh): Bill
- Moneda (moh-neh-dah): Coin
- Efectivo (eh-fehk-tee-voh): Cash
- Tarjeta de crédito (tahr-heh-tah deh kreh-dee-toh): Credit card
- Cajero automático (kah-heh-roh ow-toh-mah-tee-koh): ATM
- Cambio (kahm-bee-oh): Change
- Precio (preh-see-oh): Price
- Descuento (dehs-kwehn-toh): Discount
- Factura (fahk-too-rah): Invoice
- Recibo (reh-see-boh): Receipt

Now, let's dive into some money-related verbs and phrases:

- Pagar (pah-gahr): To pay
- Cobrar (koh-brahr): To charge or to collect payment
- Comprar (kohm-prahr): To buy
- Vender (benn-dehr): To sell
- Costar (kohs-tahr): To cost

- Ahorrar (ah-oh-hahr): To save
- Gastar (gah-stahr): To spend
- Pedir prestado (peh-deer prehs-tah-doh): To borrow
- Prestar (preh-stahr): To lend
- Devolver (deh-bohl-behr): To return (as in returning borrowed money)

And here are some additional money-related phrases that may come in handy:

- ¿Cuánto cuesta?: How much does it cost?
- Tengo suficiente dinero: I have enough money
- ¿Aceptan tarjeta de crédito?: Do you accept credit card?
- ¿Dónde está el cajero automático más cercano?: Where is the nearest ATM?
- ¿Puedo pagar con dólares/euros?: Can I pay with dollars/euros?
- Quiero cambiar dólares/euros a pesos: I want to exchange dollars/euros for pesos
- No me alcanza: I can't afford (something)
- Está en oferta: It's on sale
- No aceptamos devoluciones: We don't accept returns

Remember, talking about money may vary depending on the country or region you are in. Nevertheless, these phrases should provide you with a good foundation, but don't be afraid to ask for clarification if you are unsure! Again,

Spanish speakers love when foreign people are curious about their language.

PUNCTUATION SYMBOLS FOR EMAIL ADDRESSES

You may also be confused about some of the symbols that appear in email addresses. Here's a quick guide to help you out!

- Arroba: "@" at sign
- Punto: "." period
- Guion: "-" hyphen
- Guión bajo: "_" underscore

In Spanish, the at sign is called "arroba," which is derived from the Arabic word for "quarter." It's used in email addresses to separate the user name from the domain name.

The period, or "punto" in Spanish, is used to separate different parts of the domain name.

The hyphen, or "guion" in Spanish, is sometimes used to separate words in the user name or domain name.

Finally, the underscore, or "guión bajo" in Spanish, is also sometimes used to separate words in the user name or domain name.

Knowing these symbols will help you create and understand Spanish email addresses with ease. Keep them in mind next time you're communicating online in Spanish.

EXPRESSING LIKES AND DISLIKES

Next, we'll focus on expressing likes and dislikes in Spanish without delving into verb conjugation. By the end of this section, you'll be able to answer questions about your hobbies and interests and express whether you like or dislike certain things in both the singular and plural forms.

Vocabulary:

- Gustar (goos-tahr): To like
- Me gusta (meh goos-tah): I like
- Encantar (en-kahn-tahr): To love
- Odio (oh-dee-oh): I hate
- No me gusta (no meh goos-tah): I don't like

And here, you have some activities and things with which you can combine the previous phrases to explain your interests to a Spanish speaker.

- Los deportes (lohs deh-pohr-tehs): The sports
- La música (lah moo-see-kah): The music
- La comida (lah koh-mee-dah): The food
- Los animales (lohs ah-nee-mah-lehs): The animals
- La lectura (lah lehk-too-rah): The reading

- El cine (ehl see-neh): The movies/Cinema
- Los videojuegos (lohs bee-deh-oh-hweh-gohs): The video games
- Los viajes (lohs bee-ah-hehs): The travel
- La playa (lah plah-yah): The beach
- La montaña (lah mohn-tahn-yah): The mountain
- El campo (ehl kahm-poh): The countryside
- La ciudad (lah see-oo-dahd): The city

Let's see some expressions employing these words:

- Me gusta la música. (I like music.)
- Me encanta la playa. (I love the beach.)
- Odio los videojuegos. (I hate video games.)
- No me gusta la comida picante. (I don't like spicy food.)
- ¿Te gustan los deportes? (Do you like sports?)
- ¿Te encanta la lectura? (Do you love reading?)
- ¿Te gusta viajar? (Do you like to travel?)
- A mí no me gusta el cine. (I don't like movies.)

Keep in mind that if the thing being liked is plural, then you use the plural form of the verb (gustan, encantan, etc.).

By now, you have acquired a solid foundation for starting conversations in a wide range of situations in Spanish. You know how to greet and introduce yourself, ask about someone's well-being, tell time, make appointments or reservations, order food at a restaurant, understand money terminology, talk about the weather, and say hello and goodbye in different ways. Additionally, you've learned how to express your likes and dislikes, which can be extremely helpful in social settings. However, in order to become proficient Spanish speakers, we need to delve into the mechanics of the language. In the next chapter, we'll explore the fundamentals of Spanish grammar, including verb conjugation, noun and adjective agreement, and sentence structure. With these tools, you'll be able to take your Spanish conversations to a more meaningful level and communicate more effectively with native speakers. Let's go for it!

PRACTICE AND VOCABULARY

To help you practice using the phrases and vocabulary we've covered in the previous sections, I have created three different conversations between two people. However, I am going to delete one person's answers in each of these conversations, so that you can practice filling in the missing words and phrases. For each of the conversations, think about the situation and the relationship between the two speakers. Are they friends? Colleagues? Acquaintances? This will help you choose appropriate phrases and expressions.

Conversation 1:

Person A: ¡Hola! ¿_____?

Person B: Estoy bien, gracias. ¿Y __?

A: También estoy _____, gracias. Oye, ¿has visto la última película de acción?

B: Sí, la vi el fin de _____ pasado. Fue muy emocionante.

A: ¡Genial! ¿Te gustó?

B: ¡Sí! Me _____ ese tipo de películas.

A: ¡A mí también! ¿Vamos a ver la nueva película de terror este fin de semana al _____?

B: Claro, me encantaría.

Conversation 2:

A: ¡_____!

B: Buen día para tí también. ¿_____?

A: Regular. Oye, ¿sabes dónde puedo encontrar un buen restaurante mexicano por aquí?

B: Sí, conozco uno que está cerca. Se _____ "El Azteca". ¿Te _____ la comida mexicana?

A: Sí. Me encanta el guacamole y los tacos.

B: Ah, entonces definitivamente deberías ir a este restaurante. Tienen los mejores tacos de la ciudad.

A: ¡Gracias por la recomendación! ¡_____!.

B: ¡Adiós!

Conversation 3:

A: ¿_____?

B: Mi nombre es Adriel. Un placer. ¿Está caluroso?

A: No. En verdad esta lloviendo mucho. ¿Te gusta este clima?

B: _____, prefiero el clima soleado.

A: ¡Yo también! _____ ir a la playa cuando hace calor.

B: Interesante, yo odio la playa, _____ ir a la montaña.

A: También amo la montaña. Pero no en verano, sino en _____, cuando esta nevado.

B: ¡Genial! Bueno, ya es tarde. Debo irme. ¡_____!

After completing the exercise, you'll have a better understanding of how to use the phrases and vocabulary we've covered in real-life conversations.

Answers:

Conversation 1:

A: Cómo estas

B: tú

A: bien

B: semana

B: encantan

A: cine

Conversation 2:

A: Buen día

B: Cómo estás

B: llama; gusta

A: Hasta luego/Adiós

Conversation 3:

A: Cómo te llamas

B: No me gusta/Lo odio

A: Me gusta

B: Yo prefiero

A: invierno

B: Adiós

GETTING COMFORTABLE WITH SPANISH GRAMMAR

Now that you have built a strong foundation with vocabulary and basic phrases, it's time to take your Spanish skills to the next level by exploring the world of grammar. Don't worry if you feel intimidated by the thought of learning grammar rules; remember the old Spanish saying, "Quien tiene boca se equivoca!", which means "Who has a mouth makes mistakes."

Making mistakes is a natural part of the learning process, and the more you practice, the better you will become. So, let's dive in and get started!

PRONOUNS

Let's start with the pronouns—the fundamental basis of every sentence.

Subject pronouns:

- Yo (yoh): I
- Tú (too): You
- Él (ehl), ella (eh-yah): He/she/it
- Nosotros/nosotras (noh-soh-trohs/noh-soh-trahs): We
- Vosotros/vosotras/ustedes (boh-soh-trohs/boh-soh-trahs/oos-teh-dehs): You (plural)
- Ellos/ellas (eh-yohs/eh-yahs): They

Possessive pronouns:

- Mío/mía (mee-oh/mee-ah): Mine
- Tuyo/tuya (too-yoh/too-yah): Yours
- Suyo/suya (soo-yoh/soo-yah): His/hers
- Nuestro/nuestra (nwes-troh/nwes-trah): Ours
- Vuestro/vuestra (bwes-troh/bwes-trah): Yours (plural)
- Suyos/suyas (soo-yohs/soo-yahs): Theirs

Direct object pronouns:

- Me (meh): Me
- Te (teh): You
- Lo/La (loh/lah): Him/it, her/it
- Nos (nohs): Us
- Os (ohs): You (plural)

- Los/Las (lohs/lahs): Them

For instance: No me gusta (I don't like it); ¡Las adoro! (I adore them); Nos vamos ahora (We are going now).

Indirect object pronouns:

- Me (meh): To me
- Te (teh): To you
- Le (leh): To him, to her, to you (formal)
- Nos (nohs): To us
- Os (ohs): To you (plural)
- Les (lehs): To them

For instance: Juan me mira (Juan looks at me); Él nos faltó el respeto (He disrespected us); ¿A vosotros no os apetece venir? (Don't you feel like coming?).

Relative pronouns:

"Los pronombres relativos" in Spanish grammar are "que," "cual," "quien," "cuyo"/"cuya," "cuanto"/"cuanta" and their plural forms.

- Que (keh): That/which/who
- Cual/cuales (khu-ahl/khu-ah-lehs): Which
- Quien/quienes (kee-ehn/kee-eh-nehs): Who/whom
- Cuyo/a, cuyos/as (khu-yoh/yah, khu-yohs/yahs): Whose/which

- Cuanto/a, cuantos/as (khu-ahn-toh/tah, khu-ahn-tohs/tahs): How much/many

Indefinite pronouns:

- Alguien (ahl-gyehn): Someone
- Nadie (nah-dyeh): No one, nobody
- Algún/alguno, algunos/as (ahl-goon/ahl-goo-noh, ahl-goo-nohs/nahs): Some (singular/plural)
- Ningún/ninguno/ninguna (neen-goon/neen-goo-noh/neen-goo-nah): None, any (singular/plural)
- Cualquier/a (kwal-kee-ehr/kwal-kee-eh-rah): Whichever
- Mucho/a, muchos/as (muh-choh/ah, muh-chohs-ahs): A lot, many
- Otro/a, otros/as (oh-troh/ah, oh-trohs/ahs): Another
- Todo/a, todos/as (toh-doh/ah, toh-dohs/ahs): All, everything
- Uno/a (uh-noh/ah): One
- Varios/as (bah-ryohs/ahs): Several, many

Demonstrative pronouns:

In English there are two words: "this" and "that." In Spanish, there are three demonstrative pronouns: Two that are the same as "this" and "that," and a third that refers to an object that is farther away.

- Este/esta (ehs-teh/ehs-tah): This
- Ese/esa (eh-seh/eh-sah): That
- Aquel/aquella (ah-kehl/ah-keh-yah): That over there

NOUNS, THEIR PLURALS, AND ARTICLES

In Spanish, there are two types of articles: definite and indefinite. The definite article corresponds to "the" in English and specifies a particular noun, while the indefinite article corresponds to "a/an" in English and refers to a nonspecific noun. Here are some examples:

- El libro (the book) - definite
- La casa (the house) - definite
- Un libro (a book) - indefinite
- Una casa (a house) - indefinite

The gender of the article must correspond to the gender of the noun it is describing. By learning the rules for noun gender and article use, you'll be able to form and understand basic Spanish sentences easily. Now, check some useful vocabulary to include in your speaking:

- El hombre (ehl ohm-breh): The man
- Un muchacho (uhn muh-chah-choh): A young man
- Las chicas (lahs chee-kahs): The girls
- Una mujer (oo-nah moo-hehr): A woman
- Los niños (lohs nee-nyohs): The children

- Una escuela (oo-nah ess-kweh-lah): A school
- Las personas (lahs pehr-soh-nahs): The people

In Spanish the plural form is determined by its last letter. The general rule for forming plurals is that we add -"s" if the noun ends in a vowel and -"es" if it ends in a consonant. Here are some examples of nouns and their plurals:

- El libro (the book) → Los libros (the books)
- La casa (the house) → Las casas (the houses)
- El árbol (the tree) → Los árboles (the trees)
- La canción (the song) → Las canciones (the songs)

To determine whether a noun is masculine or feminine, there are some general patterns to look out for. For example, most nouns that end in "o" are masculine, while most nouns that end in "a" are feminine. However, there are many exceptions to this rule, so it's best to learn the gender of a noun along with its spelling.

NOUNS AND GENDERS THAT DON'T FOLLOW THE RULES

Are you tired of learning Spanish nouns and their gender rules? Well, brace yourself because some nouns just don't follow the rules! Here are two lists of Spanish nouns with irregular gender.

Masculine nouns that end in -a:

- El día (the day)
- El agua (the water)
- El mapa (the map)
- El sofa (the sofa)
- El planeta (the planet)
- El clima (the climate)

Feminine nouns that end in -o:

- La mano (the hand)
- La radio (the radio)
- La moto (the motorcycle)
- La foto (the photo)

Now, you might be thinking, "But why do these nouns break the rules?" The truth is, there is no logical explanation. These nouns just evolved over time to have a different gender than what their endings suggest. So, the best way to learn them is through practice and repetition.

Remember, learning a language is not always logical, but it can still be fun and rewarding.

ADJECTIVES

Adjectives are a fundamental part of learning Spanish, as they are used to describe people, places, things, and ideas.

Here are some of the most common adjectives you will come across:

- Feliz (feh-lees): Happy
- Triste (tree-steh): Sad
- Grande (grahn-deh): Big
- Pequeño (pek-eh-nyoh): Small
- Fuerte (foo-ehr-teh): Strong
- Débil (deh-beel): Weak
- Bonito (boh-nee-toh): Pretty
- Feo (feh-oh): Ugly
- Delgado (dehl-gah-doh): Thin
- Gordo (gohr-doh): Fat
- Inteligente (een-teh-lee-hen-teh): Intelligent
- Tonto (tohn-toh): Stupid

In Spanish, adjectives usually come after the noun they describe. However, there are some adjectives that come before the noun. Here are some rules to remember:

Adjectives of quantity or number usually come **before** the noun:

- Dos gatos negros (dohs gah-tohs neh-grohs): Two black cats
- Pocos amigos (poh-kohs ah-mee-gohs): Few friends

Adjectives of size and shape usually come **after** the noun:

- Una casa grande (oo-nah kah-sah grahn-deh): A big house
- Una mesa redonda (oo-nah meh-sah reh-dohn-dah): A round table

Adjectives of color usually come **after** the noun:

- Una camisa roja (oo-nah kah-mee-sah roh-hah): A red shirt
- Un coche azul (oon koh-cheh ah-sool): A blue car
- Un vestido blanco (oon beh-stee-doh blahn-koh): A white dress

Adjectives of personality usually come **after** the noun:

- Un hombre inteligente (oon ohm-breh een-teh-lee-hen-teh): An intelligent man
- Una pelea tonta (oo-nah peh-leh-ah tohn-tah): A stupid fight

PREPOSITIONS

Prepositions are a crucial part of any language, and Spanish has 21 prepositions in use. Let's take a look at each one and its translation, along with some examples:

- **a** (ah): to - Voy a la playa este fin de semana. (I am going to the beach this weekend.)
- **ante** (ahn-teh): before, in front of, in view of - Ante cualquier problema, llama al servicio de atención al cliente. (Before any problem, call the customer service.)
- **bajo** (bah-hoh): under, beneath, below - Los zapatos están bajo la cama. (The shoes are under the bed.)
- **con** (kohn): with - Me gusta ir al cine con mis amigos. (I like to go to the movies with my friends.)
- **contra** (kohn-trah): against - El equipo de fútbol jugó contra el equipo de baloncesto. (The soccer team played against the basketball team.)
- **de** (deh): of, from, about - La casa de mi abuela es muy grande. (My grandmother's house is very big.)
- **desde** (dehs-deh): from, since - Toco el piano desde que tenía 10 años. (I play the piano since I was 10 years old)
- **durante** (doo-rahn-teh): during - Durante el concierto, todos estaban bailando. (During the concert, everyone was dancing.)
- **en** (ehn): in, on, at - Estoy en la biblioteca estudiando para mi examen. (I am in the library studying for my exam.)
- **entre** (ehn-treh): between, among - El restaurante está entre el cine y el teatro. (The restaurant is between the movie theater and the theater.)

- **hacia** (ah-syah): towards - Caminé hacia la playa para ver el atardecer. (I walked towards the beach to see the sunset.)
- **hasta** (ahs-tah): until, up to, as far as - Caminé hasta el final de la calle. (I walked up to the end of the street.)
- **mediante** (meh-dyahn-teh): by means of, through - Se puede reservar el hotel mediante la página web. (You can book the hotel through the website.)
- **para** (pah-rah): for, in order to - Compré una tarta para el cumpleaños de mi amiga. (I bought a cake for my friend's birthday.)
- **por** (pohr): for, by, through - Hay que pronunciarse por los derechos. (You have to speak up for your rights.)
- **según** (seh-goon): according to - Según las noticias, va a llover mañana. (According to the news, it's going to rain tomorrow.)
- **sin** (seen): without - No puedo vivir sin música. (I can't live without music.)
- **sobre** (soh-breh): on, about, over - El libro trata sobre la vida de un astronauta. (The book is about the life of an astronaut.)
- **tras** (trahs): after, behind - Hay un parque tras del edificio. (There is a park behind the building.)
- **versus** (behr-soos): versus - El partido es Barcelona versus Madrid. (The game is Barcelona versus Madrid.)

- **vía** (bee-ah): via, through - El tren llega a Madrid vía Barcelona (The train arrives in Madrid via Barcelona.)

It's important to note that some verbs require specific prepositions to be used correctly. Here are some examples:

- Casarse con (kah-sahr-seh kohn): to marry [someone]
- Esperar por (eh-speh-rahr pohr): to wait for
- Hablar de (ah-blahr deh): to talk about
- Acostumbrarse a (ah-kohs-toom-brahr-seh ah): to get used to
- Depender de (deh-pehn-dehr deh): to depend on
- Soñar con (soh-nyahr kohn): to dream about
- Preguntar por (preh-goon-tahr pohr): to ask for

Learning prepositions and their corresponding verbs can be a challenge, but it's a necessary step to achieving fluency in Spanish. Remember to always study them in context and practice using them in sentences.

BASIC SENTENCE STRUCTURE

Spanish is a flexible language that allows for a lot of variation in sentence structure, but there are a few basic rules to keep in mind.

First off, let's talk about verbs. In Spanish, every verb is conjugated depending on the subject. For example, if you want to say "I cook," you would say "yo cocino." The verb "cocino" changes to match the subject pronoun "yo" (which means "I" in English). But don't worry, we'll dive deeper into verb conjugation in the next chapter.

Subject pronouns are optional in Spanish and are usually only used for emphasis. So, instead of saying "yo cocino," you could just say "cocino" to mean "I cook."

Verbs can also go before the subject for emphasis. So instead of saying "yo cocino," you would say "cocino yo" to emphasize who is doing the cooking.

Adverbs are another flexible part of Spanish sentence structure. They can go almost anywhere in a sentence, unlike in English where they usually come before the verb. For example, you could say "Rápidamente cocino la cena" (I quickly cook dinner) or "Cocino la cena rápidamente" (I cook dinner quickly).

Negative sentences require the word "no" before the verb. So, to say "I don't cook," you would say "No cocino." And don't worry, double negatives are actually the norm in Spanish, so saying "No cocino nunca" is perfectly correct, although its literal translation to English is "I don't cook never."

As I mentioned before in the book, questions in Spanish have the same structure as affirmative sentences, but with a rising intonation or by adding a tag question. For example, to ask "Do you like pizza?" you could say "¿Te gusta la pizza?" The word order is the same as in an affirmative sentence ("Te gusta la pizza"), but the rising intonation at the end makes it clear that it's a question.

As you may already notice, Spanish sentence structure is quite flexible, which allows for a lot of creativity and expression. It is a wonderful and rich language, to say the least!

In the next chapter, we'll dive into the exciting world of Spanish verbs. While it may seem daunting at first, mastering verbs is essential to becoming eloquent in Spanish. We'll start by looking at regular verbs that end in -ar, -er, and -ir. Then, we'll move on to irregular verbs and explore their unique conjugation patterns. By the end of the chapter, you'll have a solid understanding of Spanish verb conjugation and be well on your way to speaking Spanish with confidence. So, don't get discouraged, let's tackle verbs together!

PRACTICE AND VOCABULARY

1- Pronouns Quiz

A- What is the subject pronoun for "he"?

   A. Yo
   B. Tú
   C. Él
   D. Ella

B- What is the subject pronoun for "we" (all women)?

    A. Nosotros
    B. Nosotras
    C. Ellos
    D. Ellas

C- What is the possessive pronoun for "mine"?

    A. Mío/mía
    B. Tuyo/tuya
    C. Suyo/suya
    D. Nuestro/nuestra

D- What is the direct object pronoun for "her"?

    A. Me
    B. Te
    C. Lo
    D. La

Answers:

A - c)

B - b)

C - a)

D - d)

2- Fill in the blank with the correct definite article "el" or "la" (meaning "the") before the given noun. If the noun is plural, use "los" or "las" instead.

1. _____ gato (the cat)
2. _____ perro (the dog)
3. _____ casa (the house)
4. _____ coches (the cars)
5. _____ libros (the books)
6. _____ amigos (the friends)
7. _____ mesa (the table)
8. _____ silla (the chair)
9. _____ chica (the girl)
10. _____ chicos (the boys)

Answers:

1. el gato
2. el perro
3. la casa
4. los coches
5. los libros
6. los amigos
7. la mesa
8. la silla
9. la chica
10. los chicos

3- **Choose an object in the room and describe it using an adjective in Spanish. Then, try to place the adjective before and after the noun to practice the placement rules.**

4- **Prepositions Quiz:**

1. Mi hermano vive __ California.

    a) en
    b) bajo
    c) ante
    d) con

2. Voy al gimnasio _____ mi amiga.

    a) bajo
    b) mediante
    c) hacia
    d) con

3. El libro está _____ la mesa.

    a) durante
    b) por
    c) sobre
    d) sin

4. Mi cumpleaños es __ Diciembre.

a) en

b) hasta

c) con

d) según

5. Estamos caminando _____ el parque.

a) hacia

b) de

c) contra

d) bajo

6. El gato está escondido _____ la cama.

a) bajo

b) mediante

c) con

d) hacia

7. Shirley es alérgica __ los mariscos.

a) hasta

b) a

c) según

d) bajo

8. Estamos yendo _____ el norte.

   a) hasta
   b) mediante
   c) hacia
   d) bajo

9. Nuestro tren está _____ la estación 4 y 6.

   a) desde
   b) durante
   c) entre
   d) contra

10. Ellos caminan _____ el césped.

    a) bajo
    b) con
    c) hacia
    d) sobre

Answers:

1. a)
2. d)
3. c)
4. a)
5. a)

6. a)
7. b)
8. c)
9. c)
10. d)

5- Read and complete the sentences:

En aquel momento, eran las 2 de la _____(1) y yo estaba disfrutando del Día de Acción de Gracias junto a mi amiga María en un restaurante del centro. En cuanto llegamos, nos sentamos en una mesa cercana a la ventana para disfrutar de la vista de la calle.

Después de unos minutos, se nos acercó un amable _____(2). "Buenas tardes, ¿qué les gustaría pedir?" nos dijo. "¿Nos _____(3), por favor?", le preguntamos. Él nos entregó el _____(4) y, tras pensarlo un poco, decidimos compartir una entrada y un plato principal.

Mientras esperábamos la comida, María, intrigada, preguntó al mesero: "_____"(5). Él le respondió que contenía carne y verduras. A ella le gustaba la carne, pero _____(6) las verduras, mientras que a mí me encanta el pescado.

Después de la deliciosa comida, María y yo hablamos sobre nuestros planes futuros. Ella me contó que le encantaría ir a la montaña, pero a mi no me gusta mucho, porque siempre está nevado y frío. "¿_____(7) te gusta la montaña?" le pregunté. María me dijo que le gustaba la tranquilidad y los animales que se podían ver allí. Por otro lado, yo _____(8) ir a la playa y comer mariscos.

Translation:

At that time, it was 2 in the afternoon and I was enjoying Thanksgiving with my friend Maria in a downtown restaurant. As soon as we arrived, we sat at a table near the window to enjoy the view of the street.

After a few minutes, a friendly waiter approached us. "Good afternoon, what would you like to order?" He told us. "Can we get the menu, please?" we asked. He handed us the menu and, after thinking about it for a bit, we decided to share a starter and a main course.

While we were waiting for the food, María, intrigued, asked the waiter: "What's on this plate?" He replied that it contained meat and vegetables. She liked meat, but she didn't like vegetables, while I love fish.

After the delicious meal, Maria and I talked about our future plans. She told me that she would love to go to the mountains, but I don't like it very much, because it's always snowy and cold. "Why do you like the mountain?" I asked her. Maria told me that she liked the tranquility and the animals that could be seen there. On the other hand, I prefer to go to the beach and eat seafood.

Answers:

1. tarde
2. mesero
3. puede dar la carta
4. menú
5. ¿Qué lleva este plato?
6. no le gustaban
7. Por qué
8. prefiero

6- Observe and complete the following table with the gender of the nouns:

Noun	Translation	Article	Gender and Number
Allergy	Alergia	__(1)	fem. sing.
Canes	Bastones	Los	masc. pl.
Chaos	Caos	El	_____(2)
Diamonds	Diamantes	__(3)	masc. pl.
Eclipse	Eclipse	El	masc. sing.
Fissure	Fisura	La	fem. sing.
Glasses	Gafas	__(4)	fem. pl.
Hypothesis	Hipótesis	La	fem. sing.
Insects	Insectos	Los	_____(5)
Giraffes	Jirafas	Las	fem. pl.
Kermes	Kermés	__(6)	fem. sing.

Noun	Translation	Article	Gender and Number
Marble	Mármol	El	masc. sing.
Fog	Neblina	__(7)	_____(8)
Ears	Oídos	Los	masc. pl.
Pigeons	Palomas	Las	fem. pl.
Entropy	Entropía	La	fem. sing.
Butterflies	Mariposas	__(9)	fem. pl.
Keys	Llaves	Las	_____(10)
Panic	Pánico	El	masc. sing.

Answers:

1. La
2. masc. sing.
3. Los
4. Las
5. masc. pl.
6. La
7. La
8. fem. sing.
9. Las

10. fem. pl.

7- Observe the following table with masculine and feminine adjectives in the singular and in the plural:

English translation	Singular masculine	Singular feminine	Plural masculine	Plural feminine
Bitter	Amargo	Amarga	Amargos	Amargas
Careful	Cuidadoso	Cuidadosa	Cuidadosos	Cuidadosas
Clear	Claro	Clara	Claros	Claras
Dark	Oscuro	Oscura	Oscuros	Oscuras
Dirty	Sucio	Sucia	Sucios	Sucias
Easy	Fácil	Fácil	Fáciles	Fáciles
Fast	Rápido	Rápida	Rápidos	Rápidas
Fresh	Fresco	Fresca	Frescos	Frescas
Hard	Difícil	Difícil	Difíciles	Difíciles
Heavy	Pesado	Pesada	Pesados	Pesadas
High	Alto	Alta	Altos	Altas
Large	Grande	Grande	Grandes	Grandes
Light	Ligero	Ligera	Ligeros	Ligeras

English translation	Singular masculine	Singular feminine	Plural masculine	Plural feminine
Little	Pequeño	Pequeña	Pequeños	Pequeñas
Long	Largo	Larga	Largos	Largas
Low	Bajo	Baja	Bajos	Bajas
Narrow	Estrecho	Estrecha	Estrechos	Estrechas
Old	Viejo	Vieja	Viejos	Viejas
Rich	Rico	Rica	Ricos	Ricas
Short	Corto	Corta	Cortos	Cortas
Slow	Lento	Lenta	Lentos	Lentas
Small	Pequeño	Pequeña	Pequeños	Pequeñas
Strong	Fuerte	Fuerte	Fuertes	Fuertes
Tasty	Sabroso	Sabrosa	Sabrosos	Sabrosas
Thin	Delgado	Delgada	Delgados	Delgadas
Ugly	Feo	Fea	Feos	Feas
Warm	Cálido	Cálida	Cálidos	Cálidas
Wet	Mojado	Mojada	Mojados	Mojadas
White	Blanco	Blanca	Blancos	Blancas
Young	Joven	Joven	Jóvenes	Jóvenes

EVERY SENTENCE NEEDS A VERB

We know that conjugating verbs in Spanish can be quite a challenge, especially for native English speakers. But fear not, as we'll start with the basics of Spanish verbs in this chapter before moving on to more complex topics like verb tenses.

As a beginner, it's important to focus on the essentials, so we won't be covering every single verb tense that exists in Spanish (there are simply too many). Instead, we'll concentrate on the verb tenses that are most useful for a beginner. These are simple and progressive tenses (past, present, and future.)

In Spanish, there are 18 tenses in total, 6 of which are simple tenses and 12 of which are compound tenses.

The six simple tenses are the present, the imperfect, the preterite, the future, the conditional, and the imperative.

Did you know that when a group of 500 Spanish learners was asked about the most challenging aspect of learning the language, 21.64% of them said that it was conjugating verbs? Only listening and understanding native speakers proved to be more difficult! (Tell Me In Spanish, n.d.). But don't let that discourage you. With practice and patience, you'll soon be able to master the intricacies of Spanish verbs.

So, let's dive into the basics of Spanish verbs and get started on our journey to verb conjugation mastery!

REGULAR VERBS IN SPANISH

Let's start at the beginning: regular verbs in the infinitive. While in English we define an infinitive by adding the preposition "to," as in "to play," in Spanish, the infinitive is identified by its three possible endings.

All regular verbs in Spanish end in -er, -ar, or -ir. It's important to remember that the verb endings will change depending on the two letters they end in and the subject pronoun. For example, let's take a look at the verbs "hablar" (to speak), "comer" (to eat), and "vivir" (to live):

Hablar:

- Yo hablo (I speak)
- Tú hablas (You speak)
- Él/Ella/Usted habla (He/She/You formal speak)
- Nosotros/Nosotras hablamos (We speak)
- Vosotros/Vosotras habláis (You all speak)
- Ellos/Ellas/Ustedes hablan (They/You all formal speak)

Comer:

- Yo como (I eat)
- Tú comes (You eat)
- Él/Ella/Usted come (He/She/You formal eat)
- Nosotros/Nosotras comemos (We eat)
- Vosotros/Vosotras coméis (You all eat)
- Ellos/Ellas/Ustedes comen (They/You all formal eat)

Vivir:

- Yo vivo (I live)
- Tú vives (You live)
- Él/Ella/Usted vive (He/She/You formal live)
- Nosotros/Nosotras vivimos (We live)
- Vosotros/Vosotras vivís (You all live)
- Ellos/Ellas/Ustedes viven (They/You all formal live)

Now, let's take a look at some common infinitive regular verbs that end in -er, -ar, or -ir:

-**ar** verbs:

- Hablar (ah-blahr): To speak
- Cantar (kahn-tahr): To sing
- Bailar (bahy-lahr): To dance
- Estudiar (ehs-too-dee-yahr): To study
- Escuchar (ehs-koo-chahr): To listen
- Llegar (yeh-gahr): To arrive
- Preguntar (preh-goon-tahr): To ask
- Mirar (mee-rahr): To look/watch
- Trabajar (trah-bah-hahr): To work
- Tomar (toh-mahr): To take/drink

-**er** verbs:

- Comer (koh-mehr): To eat
- Beber (beh-behr): To drink
- Leer (leh-ehr): To read
- Aprender (ah-preh-ndehr): To learn
- Correr (koh-rreh-r): To run
- Vender (vehn-dehr): To sell

-**ir** verbs:

- Vivir (bee-veer): To live
- Escribir (ehs-kree-beer): To write

- Abrir (ah-breehr): To open
- Asistir (ah-see-steer): To attend
- Partir (pahr-teer): To leave/depart

"SER" AND "ESTAR"

Are you ready to learn the difference between the Spanish verbs "ser" and "estar"? These two verbs are both translated as "to be" in English, but in Spanish, they have different meanings and uses. Let's dive in and explore the **four golden rules** of when to use each one.

The first rule is that "ser" is used for permanent characteristics, while "estar" is used for temporary states. For example, "soy aburrido" means "I am boring" as in, that is my permanent personality trait. In contrast, "estoy aburrido" means "I am bored" at the moment.

The second rule is that "ser" is used for professions and nationalities, while "estar" is used for location. For example, "soy médico" means "I am a doctor," while "estoy en casa" means "I am at home."

The third rule is that "ser" is used for descriptions and characteristics, while "estar" is used for conditions and emotions. For example, "eres inteligente" means "you are intelligent" as in, that is your permanent characteristic. On the other hand, "estás cansado" means "you are tired" at the moment.

The fourth and final rule is that "ser" is used for generalizations, while "estar" is used for specifics. For example, "la comida mexicana es picante" means "Mexican food is spicy" as a generalization, while "esta salsa está picante" means "this salsa is spicy" as a specific instance.

Now that you know the rules, let's review the conjugation of "ser" and "estar" in present simple:

Ser:

- Yo soy (yoh soh-y)
- Tú eres (too eh-rehs)
- Él/Ella/Usted es (ehl/eh-yah/oos-tehd ehs)
- Nosotros/as somos (noh-soh-trohs/as soh-mohs)
- Vosotros/as sois (voh-soh-trohs/as soh-ys)
- Ellos/Ellas/Ustedes son (eh-yohs/eh-yahs/oos-teh-dehs sohn)

Estar:

- Yo estoy (yoh eh-stoy)
- Tú estás (too eh-stahs)
- Él/Ella/Usted está (ehl/eh-yah/oos-tehd eh-stah)
- Nosotros/as estamos (noh-soh-trohs/as ehs-tah-mohs)
- Vosotros/as estáis (voh-soh-trohs/as eh-stah-ys)
- Ellos/Ellas/Ustedes están (eh-yohs/eh-yahs/oos-teh-dehs ehs-tahn)

Now you're ready to start using "ser" and "estar" like a pro! Remember to apply the four golden rules and practice a ton.

IRREGULAR VERBS

Now, let's talk about every language learner's nemesis: irregular verbs. These tricky little words don't follow the usual patterns of conjugation, and that can make them a real headache for Spanish amateurs. But fear not! Once you get the hang of them, you'll be using them like a pro.

Below, you'll find a chart with some of the most common irregular verbs and their conjugations in present simple tense. Take some time to study it, and you'll be well on your way to mastery.

Personal Pronoun	Tener (to have)	Hacer (to make)	Ir (to go)	Ver (to see)	Decir (to say)	Poder (Can)
Yo	Tengo	Hago	Voy	Veo	Digo	Puedo
Tú	Tienes	Haces	Vas	Ves	Dices	Puedes
Él/Ella/Usted	Tiene	Hace	Va	Ve	Dice	Puede
Nosotros/Nosotras	Tenemos	Hacemos	Vamos	Vemos	Decimos	Podemos
Vosotros/Vosotras	Tenéis	Hacéis	Vais	Veis	Decís	Podéis
Ellos/Ellas/Ustedes	Tienen	Hacen	Van	Ven	Dicen	Pueden

Personal Pronoun	Dar (to give)	Saber (to know facts)	Conocer (to know people)	Poner (to put)	Salir (to exit)	Traer (to bring)
Yo	Doy	Sé	Conozco	Pongo	Salgo	Traigo
Tú	Das	Sabes	Conoces	Pones	Sales	Traes
Él/Ella/Usted	Da	Sabe	Conoce	Pone	Sale	Trae
Nosotros/Nosotras	Damos	Sabemos	Conocemos	Ponemos	Salimos	Traemos
Vosotros/Vosotras	Dais	Sabéis	Conocéis	Ponéis	Salís	Traéis
Ellos/Ellas/Ustedes	Dan	Saben	Conocen	Ponen	Salen	Traen

Personal Pronoun	Venir (to come)	Oír (to hear)	Caer (to fall)	Caber (to fit)	Jugar (to play)	Cerrar (to close)
Yo	Vengo	Oigo	Caigo	Quepo	Juego	Cierro
Tú	Vienes	Oyes	Caes	Cabes	Juegas	Cierras
Él/Ella/Usted	Viene	Oye	Cae	Cabe	Juega	Cierra
Nosotros/Nosotras	Venimos	Oímos	Caemos	Cabemos	Jugamos	Cerramos
Vosotros/Vosotras	Venís	Oís	Caéis	Cabéis	Jugáis	Cerráis
Ellos/Ellas/Ustedes	Vienen	Oyen	Caen	Caben	Juegan	Cierran

Personal Pronoun	Empezar (to begin)	Entender (to understand)	Pensar (to think)	Perder (to lose)	Sentir (to feel)
Yo	Empiezo	Entiendo	Pienso	Pierdo	Siento
Tú	Empiezas	Entiendes	Piensas	Pierdes	Sientes
Él/Ella/Usted	Empieza	Entiende	Piensa	Pierde	Siente
Nosotros/Nosotras	Empezamos	Entendemos	Pensamos	Perdemos	Sentimos
Vosotros/Vosotras	Empezáis	Entendéis	Pensáis	Perdéis	Sentís
Ellos/Ellas/Ustedes	Empiezan	Entienden	Piensan	Pierden	Sienten

Personal Pronoun	Costar (to cost)	Lastimar (to hurt)	Encontrar (to find)	Oler (to smell)
Yo	Cuesto	Lastimo	Encuentro	Huelo
Tú	Cuestas	Lastimas	Encuentras	Hueles
Él/Ella/Usted	Cuesta	Lastima	Encuentra	Huele
Nosotros/Nosotras	Costamos	Lastimamos	Encontramos	Olemos
Vosotros/Vosotras	Costáis	Lastimáis	Encontráis	Oléis
Ellos/Ellas/Ustedes	Cuestan	Lastiman	Encuentran	Hueles

Personal Pronoun	Recordar (to remember)	Conseguir (to get)	Elegir (to choose)	Pedir (to ask for)
Yo	Recuerdo	Consigo	Elijo	Pido
Tú	Recuerdas	Consigues	Eliges	Pides
Él/Ella/Usted	Recuerda	Consigue	Elige	Pide
Nosotros/Nosotras	Recordamos	Conseguimos	Elegimos	Pedimos
Vosotros/Vosotras	Recordáis	Conseguís	Elegís	Pedís
Ellos/Ellas/Ustedes	Recuerdan	Consiguen	Eligen	Piden

THE SIMPLE TENSES

Now, it is time to talk about the simple tenses in Spanish. Don't worry, it's as simple as it sounds. We'll start by discussing regular verbs. They are, naturally, much easier to conjugate than irregular verbs because they follow the same patterns.

Regarding the present simple, we have used it to exemplify the conjugation of verbs throughout the book: For example, when we talk about regular and irregular verbs, we conjugate the verb "hablar" (to speak) in the present simple: "yo hablo," "tu hablas," "el/ella habla..."

Here are the conjugations for the regular verb "**hablar**" in the simple past and simple future:

Simple Past:

- Yo hablé (ah-bleh): I spoke
- Tú hablaste (ah-blas-teh): You spoke
- Él/ella/usted habló (ah-bloh): He/she/you (formal) spoke
- Nosotros/nosotras hablamos (ah-blah-mohs): We spoke
- Vosotros/vosotras hablasteis (ah-blas-tays): You all spoke
- Ellos/ellas/ustedes hablaron (ah-blah-ron): They/you all (formal) spoke

Simple Future:

- Yo hablaré (ah-blah-reh): I will speak
- Tú hablarás (ah-blah-rahs): You will speak
- Él/ella/usted hablará (ah-blah-rah): He/she/you (formal) will speak
- Nosotros/nosotras hablaremos (ah-blah-reh-mohs): We will speak
- Vosotros/vosotras hablaréis (ah-blah-reh-ees): You all will speak
- Ellos/ellas/ustedes hablarán (ah-blah-rahn): They/you all (formal) will speak

Here, I present a chart with the **past simple** conjugations of the most common regular verbs:

Personal Pronoun	Hablar (to talk)	Comer (to eat)	Vivir (to live)	Bailar (to dance)	Estudiar (to study)
Yo	hablé	comí	viví	bailé	estudié
Tú	hablaste	comiste	viviste	bailaste	estudiaste
Él/Ella/Usted	habló	comió	vivió	bailó	estudió
Nosotros/Nosotras	hablamos	comimos	vivimos	bailamos	estudiamos
Vosotros/Vosotras	hablasteis	comisteis	vivisteis	bailasteis	estudiasteis
Ellos/Ellas/Ustedes	hablaron	comieron	vivieron	bailaron	estudiaron

Personal Pronoun	Trabajar (to work)	Tomar (to take/to drink)	Cantar (to sing)	Caminar (to walk)	Viajar (to travel)
Yo	trabajé	tomé	canté	caminé	viajé
Tú	trabajaste	tomaste	cantaste	caminaste	viajaste
Él/Ella/Usted	trabajó	tomó	cantó	caminó	viajó
Nosotros/Nosotras	trabajamos	tomamos	cantamos	caminamos	viajamos
Vosotros/Vosotras	trabajasteis	tomasteis	cantasteis	caminasteis	viajasteis
Ellos/Ellas/Ustedes	trabajaron	tomaron	cantaron	caminaron	viajaron

Now, observe how the same verbs are conjugated in the **simple future**:

Personal Pronoun	Hablar (to talk)	Comer (to eat)	Vivir (to live)	Bailar (to dance)	Estudiar (to study)
Yo	hablaré	comeré	viviré	bailaré	estudiaré
Tú	hablarás	comerás	vivirás	bailarás	estudiarás
Él/Ella/Usted	hablará	comerá	vivirá	bailará	estudiará
Nosotros/Nosotras	hablaremos	comeremos	viviremos	bailaremos	estudiaremos
Vosotros/Vosotras	hablaréis	comeréis	viviréis	bailaréis	estudiaréis
Ellos/Ellas/Ustedes	hablarán	comerán	vivirán	bailarán	estudiarán

Personal Pronoun	Trabajar (to work)	Tomar (to take/to drink)	Cantar (to sing)	Caminar (to walk)	Viajar (to travel)
Yo	trabajaré	tomaré	cantaré	caminaré	viajaré
Tú	trabajarás	tomarás	cantarás	caminarás	viajarás
Él/Ella/Usted	trabajará	tomará	cantará	caminará	viajará
Nosotros/Nosotras	trabajaremos	tomaremos	cantaremos	caminaremos	viajaremos
Vosotros/Vosotras	trabajaréis	tomaréis	cantaréis	caminaréis	viajaréis
Ellos/Ellas/Ustedes	trabajarán	tomarán	cantarán	caminarán	viajarán

Lastly, we have irregular verbs. These verbs don't follow regular patterns, so you'll need to memorize their conjugations. Here are some of the most common irregular verbs in **simple past**:

Personal Pronoun	Ser (to be)	Estar (to be)	Tener (to have)	Querer (to want)
Yo	Fui	Estuve	Tuve	Quise
Tú	Fuiste	Estuviste	Tuviste	Quisiste
Él/Ella/Usted	Fue	Estuvo	Tuvo	Quiso
Nosotros/Nosotras	Fuimos	Estuvimos	Tuvimos	Quisimos
Vosotros/Vosotras	Fuisteis	Estuvisteis	Tuvisteis	Quisisteis
Ellos/Ellas/Ustedes	Fueron	Estuvieron	Tuvieron	Quisieron

Personal Pronoun	Hacer (to do)	Ir (to go)	Venir (to come)	Decir (to say)
Yo	Hice	Fui	Vine	Dije
Tú	Hiciste	Fuiste	Viniste	Dijiste
Él/Ella/Usted	Hizo	Fue	Vino	Dijo
Nosotros/Nosotras	Hicimos	Fuimos	Vinimos	Dijimos
Vosotros/Vosotras	Hicisteis	Fuisteis	Vinisteis	Dijisteis
Ellos/Ellas/Ustedes	Hicieron	Fueron	Vinieron	Dijeron

Here, you have a chart with the same irregular verbs conjugated in **simple future**:

Personal Pronoun	Ser (to be)	Estar (to be)	Tener (to have)	Querer (to want)
Yo	Seré	Estaré	Tendré	Querré
Tú	Serás	Estarás	Tendrás	Querrás
Él/Ella/Usted	Será	Estará	Tendrá	Querrá
Nosotros/Nosotras	Seremos	Estaremos	Tendremos	Querremos
Vosotros/Vosotras	Seréis	Estaréis	Tendréis	Querréis
Ellos/Ellas/Ustedes	Serán	Estarán	Tendrán	Querrán

Personal Pronoun	Hacer (to do)	Ir (to go)	Venir (to come)	Decir (to say)
Yo	Haré	Iré	Vendré	Diré
Tú	Harás	Irás	Vendrás	Dirás
Él/Ella/Usted	Hará	Irá	Vendrá	Dirá
Nosotros/Nosotras	Haremos	Iremos	Vendremos	Diremos
Vosotros/Vosotras	Haréis	Iréis	Vendréis	Diréis
Ellos/Ellas/Ustedes	Harán	Irán	Vendrán	Dirán

The two most important verbs in Spanish: "ser" and "estar." They both mean "to be" and now we will learn when we are supposed to use each of them. I mentioned these verbs before and now we'll look at them in more detail.

These are both irregular verbs, which means they don't follow regular conjugation patterns. "Ser" is used to talk about permanent or long-term characteristics, while "estar" is used to talk about temporary states or conditions.

Here are the conjugations of the verb "**ser**" in the simple past and simple future:

Simple past:

- Yo fui (fwee): I was
- Tú fuiste (fwis-teh): You were
- Él/ella/usted fue (fweh): He/she/you (formal) was
- Nosotros/nosotras fuimos (fwee-mohs): We were
- Vosotros/vosotras fuisteis (fwee-stays): You all were
- Ellos/ellas/ustedes fueron (fweh-ron): They/you all (formal) were

Simple future:

- Yo seré (seh-reh): I will be
- Tú serás (seh-rahs): You will be
- Él/ella/usted será (seh-rah): He/she/you (formal) will be

- Nosotros/nosotras seremos (seh-reh-mohs): We will be
- Vosotros/vosotras seréis (seh-reh-ees): You all will be
- Ellos/ellas/ustedes serán (seh-rahn): They/you all (formal) will be

If you have any doubts about the pronunciation of the letter "r" in these words, take a quick look at the first chapter, where we addressed its correct pronunciation.

Here are the conjugations of the Spanish verb "**estar**" in the simple past and simple future tenses:

Simple past:

- Yo estuve (ehs-too-veh)
- Tú estuviste (ehs-too-vees-teh)
- Él/Ella/Usted estuvo (ehs-too-boh)
- Nosotros/Nosotras estuvimos (ehs-too-vee-mohs)
- Vosotros/Vosotras estuvisteis (ehs-too-vees-tays)
- Ellos/Ellas/Ustedes estuvieron (ehs-too-byeh-rohn)

Simple future:

- Yo estaré (ehs-tah-reh)
- Tú estarás (ehs-tah-rahs)
- Él/Ella/Usted estará (ehs-tah-rah)
- Nosotros/Nosotras estaremos (ehs-tah-reh-mohs)
- Vosotros/Vosotras estaréis (ehs-tah-reys)

- Ellos/Ellas/Ustedes estarán (ehs-tah-rahn)

Remember: "Yo fui" means "I was" and "yo estuve" also means "I was" in Spanish, but the first one is used for permanent states and "yo estuve" is used for temporary states. Similarly, "yo seré" and "yo estaré" both mean "I will be" in Spanish. In the same way, the first one is used for permanent situations while the second one is used for temporary situations. If you need a reminder of how to correctly use these two important verbs, just go back quickly to check the golden rules!

Here you have some examples:

- Yo estuve de vacaciones en los Estados Unidos cuando tenía 7 años. (I was on vacation in the United States when I was 7 years old.)
- Yo fui el presidente de mi clase dos años consecutivos. (I was the president of my class two years in a row).
- Tú serás el mejor de tu clase. (You will be the best in your class).
- Mis padres estarán de viaje el próximo mes. (My parents will be traveling next month).

THE PROGRESSIVE TENSES

Are you ready to take your Spanish skills to the next level? Then let's talk about the progressive tenses.

First, let's clarify the difference between the present participle and the gerund. In English, the present participle is used with the verb "to be" to describe actions that are happening in the moment or near future, for example, "I am learning," or "I am going there next weekend."

The gerund, on the other hand, is a noun and can be used as the subject or object of a sentence, for example, "Swimming is fun" or "She loves swimming."

In Spanish, both the present participle and the gerund are referred to as "gerundio." The present participle or gerund in Spanish is formed by adding "-ando" or "-iendo" to the stem of the verb, for example, "hablando" (talking) or "comiendo" (eating). It can be used in the same way as in English, to describe actions that are happening at the moment, for example, "Estoy hablando" (I am talking).

As in English, it can function as an object. For example, "Caminando se llega lejos" (Walking gets you far). In this example, the nuclear verb is "llega" (arrive). That's the action the subject does. "Caminando" is the object, in the sense that it is a means to arrive "lejos" (far).

So, the gerund in Spanish is rather an action taking place in the present moment ("Estoy hablando") or an object (Hablando se entiende la gente.)

And here are some examples of verbs in their gerund form:

- Com**iendo** (koh-mee-ehn-doh): Eating
- Camin**ando** (kah-mee-nahn-doh): Walking
- Escrib**iendo** (eh-skree-bee-ehn-doh): Writing

But what if the verb (from -"er" and -"ir" group) has a **vowel before the termination**? In this case, you just add -"yendo." For example, the present participle of "leer" (to read) is "leyendo" (reading), and the present participle of "construir" (to build) is "construyendo" (building).

- Ir (eer): Yendo (going) - Exception
- Oír (oh-eer): Oyendo (hearing) - Add "yendo" since there's a vowel before the termination "ir."
- Decir (deh-seer): Diciendo (saying) - Add "iendo" since there's a consonant before the termination "ir."
- Hacer (ah-sehr): Haciendo (doing) - Add "iendo" since there's a consonant before the termination "er."
- Ser (sehr): Siendo (being) - Add "iendo" since there's a consonant before the termination "er."
- Venir (beh-neer): Viniendo (coming) - Add "iendo" since there's a consonant before the termination "ir."

However, not all verbs follow this pattern. Some of them have irregular present participles. You'll learn them by practicing and the more you get familiar with the language, the more you'll be able to identify exceptions.

Now that you know how to form present participles, you can use them to create the present progressive tense, also known as the present continuous tense. This tense is used to describe an action that is currently in progress.

To form the present progressive tense in Spanish, you need to use the verb "estar" (to be) in the present tense, followed by the present participle of the verb you want to use. For example, "I am eating" would be "Estoy comiendo" (ess-toy coh-mee-en-doh).

You can also use the past and future progressive tenses by using the imperfect and future tenses of "estar," respectively, followed by the present participle of the verb. For example, "I was eating" would be "Estaba comiendo" (ess-tah-bah coh-mee-en-doh), and "I will be eating" would be "Estaré comiendo" (ess-tah-reh coh-mee-en-doh).

Let me give you some examples:

- Estoy hablando por teléfono. (I am talking on the phone.)
- Estábamos caminando por el parque cuando empezó a llover. (We were walking in the park when it started raining.)

- Voy a estar estudiando para mi examen toda la noche. (I am going to be studying for my exam all night.)
- Está bailando muy bien. (He/She is dancing very well.)
- Estuvieron durmiendo toda la tarde después de la fiesta. (They were sleeping all afternoon after the party.)

You may be thinking that the present progressive is the same and indistinguishable from the gerund or participle. Let me briefly explain the difference:

In both Spanish and English, the gerund or participle is the word that ends in "ando/iendo" for Spanish, or "ing" in English. Meanwhile, the present progressive is the grammatical construction that indicates an event that is taking place in the present.

The sentence "estamos comiendo" (we are eating) is in the present progressive, where the gerund/participle is "comiendo." But the sentence could be also conjugated in the past progressive: "estabamos comiendo" (we were eating), and the gerund/participle would remain the same: "comiendo."

So, practice forming present participles and using them in the present, past, and future progressive tenses to take your Spanish verb conjugation skills to the next level!

TENER: VERB AND PHRASES

Next, we are going to talk about one of the most important and versatile verbs in the Spanish language, "tener." This verb has many uses beyond just meaning "to have," which is its most common translation. Let's explore some of the different ways to use it.

Firstly, let's look at some common expressions with "tener":

- Tener hambre (teh-ner ahm-breh): to be hungry
- Tener sed (teh-ner sehd): to be thirsty
- Tener frío/calor (teh-ner free-oh/kah-lohr): to be cold/hot
- Tener miedo (teh-ner mee-eh-doh): to be afraid
- Tener sueño (teh-ner sweh-nyoh): to be sleepy

Another important use of this verb is to express age:

- Tengo veinticinco años (tehn-goh veh-een-tee-seen-coh ahn-yohs): I am twenty-five years old.

Finally, let's talk about "tener que" (teh-ner keh), which means "to have to" or "must" in English. This phrase is used to express obligation or necessity.

For example:

- Tengo que estudiar (tehn-goh keh eh-stoo-dee-ahr): I have to study.
- No tengo que trabajar mañana (noh tehn-goh keh trah-bah-jahr mah-nyah-nah): I don't have to work tomorrow.
- ¿Tienes que ir al médico? (tyeh-nes keh eer ahl meh-dee-koh): Do you have to go to the doctor?

Remember, this is a very important verb in Spanish, not only to express possession, but also to talk about feelings, age, and obligations.

By now, you've probably noticed that Spanish verbs can be a bit of a challenge to master, but don't worry, I'm here to help you understand the perfect tenses.

To form the perfect tenses, you'll need to use the auxiliary verb "haber" and the past participle of the main verb. But wait, what is "haber"? You might remember that haber is one of the translations for "have" in Spanish, but when used as an auxiliary verb, it means "have" in the sense of "have done something."

THE PERFECT TENSES

Let's take a look at how to conjugate haber in the indicative present, imperfect, and future tenses:

- **Indicative present:** he, has, ha, hemos, habéis, han
- **Indicative imperfect:** había, habías, había, habíamos, habíais, habían
- **Indicative future**: habré, habrás, habrá, habremos, habréis, habrán

Now, let's move on to the past participle. In Spanish, there are two different sets of past participles, depending on the last two letters of the verb.

1. Verbs that end in -"ar": The past participle is formed by replacing -"ar" with -"**ado**":

- "hablar" (ah-blahr) becomes "hablado" (ah-blah-doh) (spoken)
- "caminar" (kah-mee-nahr) becomes "caminado" (kah-mee-nah-doh) (walked)
- "cantar" (kahn-tahr) becomes "cantado" (kahn-tah-doh) (sung)
- "estudiar" (ehs-too-dee-ahr) becomes "estudiado" (ehs-too-dee-ah-doh) (studied)
- "mirar" (mee-rahr) becomes "mirado" (mee-rah-doh) (watched)

- "nadar" (nah-dahr) becomes "nadado" (nah-dah-doh) (swam)
- "jugar" (hoo-gahr) becomes "jugado" (hoo-gah-doh) (played)
- "bailar" (bahy-lahr) becomes "bailado" (bahy-lah-doh) (danced)
- "viajar" (byah-hahr) becomes "viajado" (byah-hah-doh) (traveled)
- "cocinar" (koh-see-nahr) becomes "cocinado" (koh-see-nah-doh) (cooked)

2. **Verbs that end in** -"**er**" or -"**ir**": The past participle is formed by replacing them with -"**ido**."

- "comer" (koh-mehr) becomes "comido" (koh-mee-doh) (eaten)
- "vivir" (bee-beer) becomes "vivido" (bee-bee-doh) (lived)
- "beber" (beh-behr) becomes "bebido" (beh-bee-doh) (drunk)
- "correr" (koh-rreh-r) becomes "corrido" (koh-ree-doh) (run)
- "leer" (leh-ehr) becomes "leído" (leh-ee-doh) (read)
- "decidir" (deh-see-deer) becomes "decidido" (deh-see-dee-doh) (decided)
- "partir" (pahr-teer) becomes "partido" (pahr-tee-doh) (divided)

- "recibir" (reh-see-beer) becomes "recibido" (reh-see-bee-doh) (received)
- "subir" (soo-beer) becomes "subido" (soo-bee-doh) (gone up)
- "salir" (sah-leer) becomes "salido" (sah-lee-doh) (gone out)

Now that you know how to form the past participle, it's time to learn about some common irregular past participles in Spanish.

Here are some of the most common ones:

- "cubrir" (koo-breer) becomes "cubierto" (koo-bee-ehr-toh) (covered)
- "decir" (deh-seer) becomes "dicho" (dee-choh) (said)
- "escribir" (eh-skree-beer) becomes "escrito" (eh-skree-toh) (written)
- "hacer" (ah-sehr) becomes "hecho" (eh-choh) (done/made)
- "morir" (moh-reer) becomes "muerto" (moo-ehr-toh) (died)
- "poner" (poh-neer) becomes "puesto" (poo-ehs-toh) (put)
- "romper" (rohm-pehr) becomes "roto" (roh-toh) (broken)
- "ver" (vehr) becomes "visto" (vee-stoh) (seen)
- "volver" (vohl-vehr) becomes "vuelto" (voo-ehl-toh) (returned)

Now that you have a better understanding of the perfect tenses in Spanish, it's time to start practicing! Try forming some sentences using the perfect tenses with different verbs and subjects based on the following examples:

- Juan ha corrido una maratón. (Juan has run a marathon.)
- Mis hermanas habían decidido ir a la fiesta. (My sisters had decided to go to the party.)
- En los próximos meses, habrás escrito un libro. (In the next few months, you will have written a book.)

Good luck!

REFLEXIVE VERBS

Let's move on to the last topic (I promise) related to conjugations and tenses in Spanish: reflexive verbs.

Reflexive verbs are verbs that are used to indicate that the action is being performed on oneself. In other words, the subject is performing the action to or for themselves. This is done by adding a reflexive pronoun before the verb. There are six reflexive pronouns in Spanish:

- me
- te
- se
- nos

- os
- se

The reflexive pronoun used will depend on the subject performing the action. For example, if the subject is "yo" (I), the reflexive pronoun used would be "me." If the subject is "él" (he), the reflexive pronoun used would be "se."

Reflexive pronouns can be placed before the verb or can be attached to the end of an infinitive verb or present participle. For example, "me lavo" (I wash myself) or "lavarme" (to wash myself).

Reflexive verbs can be grouped into three categories:

Daily routine actions such as bathing, getting dressed, and brushing teeth.

- Levantarse (leh-bahn-TAHR-seh): To get up
- Ducharse (doo-CHAHR-seh): To take a shower
- Maquillarse (mah-kee-YAHHR-seh): To put on makeup

Actions performed on **parts of the body**.

- Peinarse (peh-ee-NAHR-seh): To comb one's hair
- Afeitarse (ah-fay-TAHR-seh): To shave
- Pintarse las uñas (peen-TAHR-seh lahs OO-nyahs): To paint one's nails

Actions done **for oneself** or **to oneself**.

- Acordarse (ah-kor-DAHR-seh): To remember
- Sentarse (sehn-TAHR-seh): To sit down
- Divertirse (dee-vehr-TEER-seh): To have fun

I know: you feel lost. You think that Spanish is too overwhelming and that you will never be able to learn all those tenses and conjugations. I understand you because, believe it or not, even for Spanish speakers it is complicated! How many times has my Spanish teacher corrected me in class for misconjugating the verbs in my sentences? In my own mother tongue!

But don't be discouraged. Learning a language is a task that requires a lot of commitment and energy, not for nothing it takes us at least the first six years of our lives to learn to communicate effectively in our mother tongue.

Let me tell you a story about someone like you, who felt the same way you are feeling now about learning Spanish. His name is Carl.

Carl is a language learner who was feeling completely overwhelmed by the vast number of Spanish verbs to learn. He couldn't believe that even the most basic verbs like "am," "are," and "is" had 12 different forms in the present tense alone! Carl was feeling defeated and frustrated, thinking that he would never be able to master the language.

But he was determined not to give up. He decided to take matters into his own hands and come up with a creative solution. He created color-coded flashcards for each verb tense and recorded himself saying different conjugations of the verbs. This way, he could listen to the recordings while he went about his daily routine, doing chores or commuting to work.

Slowly but surely, Carl started to see improvement. He could recognize patterns in verb conjugations and was able to use the correct form more often. He no longer felt overwhelmed, and he was excited to see how much more he could improve.

Carl's experience is relatable to many language learners who feel overwhelmed by the complexity of Spanish verbs. But with determination, creativity, and a little bit of hard work, anyone can master these tricky language elements.

Throughout this chapter, you have explored all the important verb conjugations to be able to express yourself profoundly in Spanish.

On this path, social faux pas can be detrimental to our confidence, but with an appreciation for Spanish culture, we can better understand and communicate with Spanish people. By finding common ground and conversation starters, we can create meaningful connections and improve our language skills. In the final chapter, we will delve deeper into Spanish culture and customs, and how they impact the language. Stay tuned for more insights and tips on mastering Spanish!

PRACTICE AND VOCABULARY

1- Order the following sentences:

1. los/ juega / mi hermano / videojuegos

   _____

2. voy / tarde / a / la universidad / siempre

   _____

3. los pájaros /cantan / en / árboles / los

   _____

4. habla / ella / con / su amiga / por teléfono

   _____

5. un libro / leemos / en la biblioteca / nosotros

   _____

6. nosotros / prepara / mi madre / la cena / para

   _____

7. corren / niños / en el parque / los

   _____

8. escucha / él/ en su habitación / la música

   _____

9. trabajan / maestros / en la escuela / los

_____

10. el perro / en el jardín / su comida / siempre / come

_____

Answers:

1. Mi hermano juega los videojuegos. (My brother plays video games.)
2. Siempre voy tarde a la universidad. (I'm always late for university.)
3. Los pájaros cantan en los árboles. (The birds sing in the trees.)
4. Ella habla con su amiga por teléfono. (She talks to her friend on the phone.)
5. Nosotros leemos un libro en la biblioteca. (We read a book in the library.)
6. Mi madre prepara la cena para nosotros. (My mother prepares dinner for us.)
7. Los niños corren en el parque. (The children run in the park.)
8. Él escucha la música en su habitación. (He listens to music in his room.)
9. Los maestros trabajan en la escuela. (The teachers work at the school.)
10. El perro come su comida siempre en el jardín. (The dog always eats his food in the garden.)

2- Conjugate the following verbs in the simple tenses with the correct pronoun, either "ser" or "estar":

1. Yo _____ en casa. (estar; past)
2. Ella _____ muy simpática. (ser; present)
3. Tú _____ de España, ¿verdad? (ser; present)
4. Nosotros _____ en la playa. (estar; future)
5. Vosotros _____ muy cansados. (estar; past)
6. Ustedes _____ mis amigos. (ser; present)
7. Él no _____ muy feliz. (estar; past)
8. Yo no _____ seguro. (estar; future)
9. Ellas _____ enfermas. (estar; future)
10. Usted _____ muy amable conmigo. (ser; present)

Answers:

1. estuve
2. es
3. eres
4. estaremos
5. estuvisteis
6. son
7. estuvo
8. estaré
9. estarán
10. es

3- Complete the following sentences with the correct form of the verb in parentheses in the progressive tense:

1. Yo _____ (hablar) con mi amigo en este momento. (present)
2. Tú _____ (bailar) en la fiesta de anoche. (past)
3. Él _____ (comer) en el restaurante a las ocho de la noche. (past)
4. Nosotros _____ (estudiar) en la biblioteca hoy en la tarde. (present)
5. Vosotros _____ (leer) el libro en este momento. (present)
6. Ellos _____ (jugar) al fútbol todos los sábados. (present)
7. Yo _____ (cantar) en el karaoke con mis amigos mañana por la noche. (future)
8. Tú y yo _____ (bailar) en la discoteca la próxima semana. (future)
9. Ella _____ (ver) la televisión a esta hora. (present)
10. Ustedes _____ (escribir) un correo electrónico en este momento. (present)

Answers:

1. estoy hablando
2. estuviste bailando
3. estuvo comiendo
4. estamos estudiando

5. estáis leyendo
6. están jugando
7. estaré cantando
8. estaremos bailando
9. está viendo
10. están escribiendo

4- Translate the following sentences into Spanish. I added the verbal tense and number to make it easier for you to identify the correct translation:

1. I have a dog. (Present simple)

_____

2. They will have a party next week. (Future simple)

_____

3. She had a headache yesterday. (Past simple)

_____

4. You have a lot of books. (Present simple, plural)

_____

5. We will have to work late tonight. (Future simple, plural)

_____

6. He had a nice car when he was young. (Past simple)

_____

7. I have to study for the exam. (Present simple)

_____

8. She will have a baby in a few months. (Future simple)

_____

9. They have a great relationship. (Present simple, plural)

_____

10. I had a good time at the party last night. (Past simple)

_____

Answers:

1. Tengo un perro.
2. Tendrán una fiesta la próxima semana.
3. Ella tuvo dolor de cabeza ayer.
4. Tienes muchos libros.
5. Tendremos que trabajar hasta tarde esta noche.
6. Él tuvo un coche bonito cuando era joven.
7. Tengo que estudiar para el examen.
8. Ella tendrá un bebé en unos meses.
9. Ellos tienen una gran relación.
10. Me divertí en la fiesta anoche.

5- Read and complete the translation:

Estaba navegando en mi barco hacia una isla desconocida, cuando de repente una tormenta se desató y el mar comenzó a agitarse violentamente. Mientras luchaba por mantener el rumbo, mi brújula se rompió y perdí toda noción de la dirección. Después de varias horas de luchar contra los elementos, finalmente avisté una costa rocosa y decidí atracar mi barco en la playa.

Una vez en tierra, empecé a explorar la isla y me di cuenta de que estaba completamente desierta. No había señales de vida humana en ninguna parte, pero encontré una cueva oculta en una colina cercana. Decidí investigar y encontré una cámara secreta llena de tesoros antiguos, pero también descubrí que la isla estaba habitada por una tribu de nativos hostiles.

A medida que exploraba más, encontré un mapa que mostraba la ubicación de un tesoro aún mayor. Sin embargo, pronto me di cuenta de que estaba siendo perseguido por los nativos. Luché por mi vida para escapar de aquella selvática jungla y regresar a mi barco, pero nunca olvidaré mi aventura en esa misteriosa isla solitaria.

Ahora, de vuelta en mi hogar, me pregunto qué habría pasado si hubiera permanecido más tiempo en la isla. ¿Habría encontrado el tesoro y escapado de los nativos? ¿O habría sido capturado y convertido en su prisionero para siempre? Todavía me pregunto qué secretos más podría haber descubierto en esa isla misteriosa.

Mirando hacia el futuro, me doy cuenta de que nunca sabré la respuesta a esas preguntas. Pero eso no significa que deba dejar de explorar y descubrir nuevos lugares. La próxima vez que zarpe hacia lo desconocido, estaré mejor preparado para enfrentar cualquier desafío que se presente. Quién sabe qué aventuras esperan en el horizonte, pero estoy listo para descubrirlas.

Translation:

I was sailing on my ship to an_____ ____(1), when suddenly a storm _____(2) and the sea _____ __ ___(3) violently. As I struggled to ____(4) on course, my compass broke and _ ___(5) all sense of direction. After several hours of fighting the elements, I finally spotted a rocky shoreline and decided to dock my boat on the____(6).

Once on land, I began __ _____(7) the island and realized that it was completely deserted. There were no signs of human life anywhere, but I __ ___(8) a hidden cave in a nearby hill. I decided to investigate and found a secret chamber full of ancient treasures, but also _____(9) that the island was inhabited by a tribe of hostile natives.

As I explored further, _ ____ _____(10) a map that showed the location of an even bigger treasure. However, I ____(11) realized that I was being persecuted by the natives. I fought for my life to escape from that jungle and return to my ship, but I ___(12) never forget my adventure on that mysterious lonely island.

Now, back home, I wonder what ____ ____(13) happened if I had stayed longer on the island. Would I have found the treasure and escaped from the natives? Or would I have been _____(14) and made their prisoner forever? I still wonder what more secrets I could have _____(15) on that mysterious island.

_____(16) to the future, I realize that I will never ____ __ _____(17) to those questions. But that doesn't mean I should stop exploring and discovering new places. The next time I set sail into the unknown, _ ___(18) be better prepared to face any challenge that comes my way. Who knows what adventures await on the horizon, but I'm ready to discover them.

Answers:

1. unknown island
2. broke out
3. began to rage
4. stay
5. I lost
6. beach
7. to explore
8. did find
9. Discovered
10. I came across

11. soon
12. will
13. would have
14. captured
15. discovered
16. Looking
17. know the answer
18. I will

6- To expand and complete your vocabulary, you will need adverbs. Observe the following table with adverbs of place, time, manner, quantity, affirmation, negation, and doubt:

Category (Categoría)	Adverb (Adverbio)
Place (Lugar)	aquí (here), allí (there), ahí (there), arriba (up), abajo (down), adentro (inside), afuera (outside), lejos (far), cerca (near)
Time (Tiempo)	ahora (now), antes (before), después (after), temprano (early), tarde (late), pronto (soon), ya (already), todavía (still), nunca (never)
Manner (Modo)	bien (well), mal (badly), lentamente (slowly), rápidamente (quickly), suavemente (softly), fuertemente (strongly), fácilmente (easily), difícilmente (difficulty), claramente (clearly)

Category (Categoría)	Adverb (Adverbio)
Quantity (Cantidad)	mucho (much/many), poco (little/few), más (more), menos (less), demasiado (too much), suficiente (enough), casi (almost), apenas (hardly), todo (all/everything)
Affirmation (Afirmación)	sí (yes), ciertamente (certainly), claro (of course), efectivamente (indeed), verdaderamente (truly), obviamente (obviously), también (also), incluso (even), siempre (always)
Negation (Negación)	no (no), nunca (never), jamás (never), tampoco (neither), ningún (none), nada (nothing), nadie (nobody), apenas (barely), apenas (barely/hardly)
Doubt (Duda)	quizás (perhaps), tal vez (maybe), posiblemente (possibly), acaso (possibly), quizá (maybe), seguramente (surely), probablemente (probably), realmente (really), casi (almost)

Usage examples:

- Voy a dejar el libro **aquí**. (I'm going to leave the book here.)
- Mañana **temprano** tengo una reunión importante. (Early tomorrow I have an important meeting.)
- La música sonaba **suavemente** en el fondo. (The music was playing softly in the background.)
- Comí **demasiado** y ahora me siento mal. (I ate too much and now I feel sick.)
- Sí, **definitivamente** quiero ir contigo. (Yes, I definitely want to go with you.)
- No, **nunca** he estado en ese restaurante. (No, I've never been to that restaurant.)

- **Tal vez** deberíamos llamar a alguien para que nos ayude. (Maybe we should call someone to help us.)
- **Quizás** ella tenga la respuesta que estamos buscando. (Perhaps she has the answer we're looking for.)
- **Probablemente** lleguemos **tarde** si no nos apuramos. (We'll probably be late if we don't hurry.)
- **Realmente no** entiendo lo que está pasando. (I really don't understand what's going on.)

7- Conjugate the following verbs according to the given instructions:

a. Conjugate the verb "aprender" (to learn) in the present simple tense for "tú," "nosotros/nosotras," and "ustedes."

_____

_____

_____

b. Conjugate the verb "correr" (to run) in the progressive past tense for "yo," "él/ella/usted," and "ellos/ellas/ustedes."

_____

_____

_____

c. Conjugate the verb "escribir" (to write) in the progressive future tense for "tú," "vosotros/vosotras," and "ustedes."

_____

_____

_____

d. Conjugate the verb "hacer" (to do/make) in the future simple tense for "yo," "él/ella/usted," and "nosotros/nosotras."

_____

_____

_____

e. Conjugate the verb "decir" (to say) in the future simple tense for "tú," "nosotros/nosotras," and "ustedes."

_____

_____

_____

f. Conjugate the verb "tener" (to have) in the present simple tense for "yo," "vosotros/vosotras," and "ellos/ellas/ustedes."

_____

_____

_____

g. Conjugate the verb "poner" (to put/place) in the past simple for "tú," "nosotros/nosotras," and "ustedes."

_____

_____

_____

h. Conjugate the verb "venir" (to come) in the present simple tense for "yo," "nosotros/nosotras," and "ellos/ellas/ustedes."

_____

_____

_____

Answers:

a. Tú: aprendes
Nosotros/nosotras: aprendemos
Ustedes: aprenden

b. Yo: estuve corriendo
Él/ella/usted: estuvo corriendo
Ellos/ellas/ustedes: estuvieron corriendo

c. Tú: estarás escribiendo
Vosotros/vosotras: estareis escribiendo
Ustedes: estarán escribiendo

d. Yo: haré
Él/ella/usted: hará
Nosotros/nosotras: haremos

e. Tú: dirás
Nosotros/nosotras: diremos
Ustedes: dirán

f. Yo: tengo
Vosotros/vosotras: tenéis
Ellos/ellas/ustedes: tienen

g. Tú: pusiste
Nosotros/nosotras: pusimos
Ustedes: pusieron

h. Yo: vengo
Nosotros/nosotras: venimos
Ellos/ellas/ustedes: vienen

8- Translate the following sentences:

a. Me levanto temprano todas las mañanas y corro en el parque cercano.

_____

b. Los niños están jugando tranquilamente en la sala de estar.

_____

c. Ayer fui al supermercado y compré todos los ingredientes para preparar una cena deliciosa.

_____

d. Si llueve esta tarde, no podré ir al concierto que tanto esperaba.

_____

e. Mañana tendré una reunión importante en la oficina y tengo que preparar mi presentación.

_____

f. Durante las vacaciones de verano, viajaré por Europa y conoceré muchas ciudades nuevas.

_____

g. Hace años que no visito a mis abuelos, debería llamarlos para organizar un encuentro.

_____

h. No entiendo por qué mi jefe siempre está tan enojado, tal vez debería hablar con él para averiguar qué pasa.

_____

i. Me encanta la música clásica, siempre la escucho mientras trabajo en mi escritorio.

_____

j. Los estudiantes están estudiando arduamente para el examen final de la materia.

_____

k. Ayer recibí una carta de mi mejor amigo que vive en otro país, me hizo muy feliz leerla.

_____

l. Esta noche saldré a cenar con mi pareja a un restaurante nuevo que abrieron en el centro.

_____

m. Siempre trato de ser amable con las personas que conozco, creo que es importante tener una actitud positiva.

_____

n. En el parque hay muchas flores de colores diferentes, me encanta caminar por allí y admirarlas.

_____

o. Si gano la lotería, me compraré una casa en la playa y pasaré el resto de mi vida relajándome bajo el sol.

_____

Answers:

a. I wake up early every morning and run in the nearby park.

b. The children are playing quietly in the living room.

c. Yesterday I went to the supermarket and bought all the ingredients to prepare a delicious dinner.

d. If it rains this afternoon, I won't be able to go to the concert that I was looking forward to.

e. Tomorrow, I will have an important meeting at the office and I have to prepare my presentation.

f. During the summer vacation, I will travel around Europe and visit many new cities.

g. It's been years since I last visited my grandparents. I should call them to arrange a meeting.

h. I don't understand why my boss is always so angry. Maybe I should talk to him to find out what's going on.

i. I love classical music. I always listen to it while I work at my desk.

j. The students are studying hard for the final exam of the subject.

k. Yesterday, I received a letter from my best friend who lives in another country. It made me very happy to read it.

l. Tonight, I will go out to dinner with my partner at a new restaurant that opened downtown.

m. I always try to be kind to people I meet. I think it's important to have a positive attitude.

n. In the park there are many flowers of different colors, I love walking around and admiring them.

o. If I win the lottery, I will buy a house on the beach and spend the rest of my life relaxing under the sun.

7

SPANISH CULTURE AND CUSTOMS

Welcome to the last chapter of this book. You have explored the unknown lands of this wonderful language so far. As a last stop on our adventure, we will dive into the fascinating world of Spanish culture and customs. Understanding cultural differences is crucial to effectively communicating and building relationships with native speakers. So, let's get started!

Picture this: our protagonist, Sarah, traveled to Mexico to attend a funeral. She arrived wearing all black, as one does for a funeral, but to her surprise, everyone else was dressed casually and in colorful clothes. She immediately felt out of place and self-conscious. To make matters worse, when she was greeted by locals with two kisses, she had no idea what was going on. She felt embarrassed and wished she had done her research beforehand.

This scenario is a perfect example of why it's important to be aware of cultural customs when traveling or communicating with native speakers. It is time to explore some of the customs and traditions of Spanish-speaking countries, including greetings, holidays, and social norms. I will also provide you with valuable advice on how to immerse yourself in the culture and take away more from your experiences. So, let's jump in and learn how to navigate cultural contrasts like a pro!

SPANISH ACCENTS AND DIALECTS

First of all, let's talk about Spanish accents and dialects! Do you know how in English, there are different accents and even different vocabulary in different countries? Well, the same goes for Spanish. For example, if you go to Spain, you might find it challenging to understand someone from Andalusia if you're used to standard Castilian Spanish. The accent can be quite different, and some words may have different meanings depending on where you are. The grammar and even the intonation of sentences can vary depending on the region.

But don't worry, this doesn't mean that learning Spanish is difficult or pointless. Just like British people understand American people despite the differences in vocabulary and accent, Spanish speakers across the globe are aware of the differences and can still understand one another. Plus, learning the different accents and dialects can even make you more proficient in the language and give you a deeper understanding of Spanish culture. So, embrace the variety, and who knows, you might even find a new favorite accent.

While Spanish is the official language in more than 20 countries around the world, today we will take a closer look at some of the most representative ones. From the vibrant street markets of Colombia to the Spanish ham, each country has its own unique identity and charm.

Let's start with Mexico, a country that has captivated visitors with its delicious food, rich history, and colorful traditions. Mexicans are known for their warm hospitality and friendly nature, making it easy for visitors to feel at home. The country is also famous for its mariachi music and intricate Day of the Dead celebrations.

Colombia, on the other hand, boasts a diverse landscape of mountains, beaches, and rainforests. Colombians are passionate about their music and dance, with cumbia and salsa being popular genres. The country is also known for its coffee production and vibrant street art scene.

Moving north, the United States is home to a large Spanish-speaking population, particularly in states like California, Texas, and New Mexico. While each community has its unique cultural identity, they all share a love for spicy food, music, and traditions like the quinceañera and Día de los Muertos.

Argentina, famous for its delicious meat, premium football, and mate drink, is a country with a strong European influence. Argentinians are proud of their meat-based cuisine and love to socialize over a traditional asado (barbecue). The capital city of Buenos Aires is also a hub for arts and culture, with many theaters, museums, and galleries.

Spain, the birthplace of the Spanish language, is a country steeped in history and tradition. Spaniards are passionate about their food and wine, with each region having its own unique culinary specialties. Flamenco music and dance are also essential parts of the country's cultural heritage.

Peru, known for its ancient Incan ruins and stunning landscapes, is a country with a rich history and culture. Peruvians are proud of their culinary traditions, with dishes like ceviche and lomo saltado gaining popularity around the world. The country is also famous for its vibrant festivals and celebrations, like Inti Raymi and Carnaval de Cajamarca.

Venezuela, with its tropical beaches and vibrant nightlife, is a country with a strong Caribbean influence. Venezuelans are passionate about their music and dance, with genres like salsa and reggaeton being especially popular. The country is also known for its oil production and traditional crafts like hammock weaving.

Chile, a narrow strip of land on the western coast of South America, is a country with a diverse landscape that includes the Andes Mountains, the Atacama Desert, and, of course, the Pacific Ocean. Chileans are proud of their wine production and love to celebrate with traditional dishes like empanadas and pastel de choclo.

Ecuador, located on the equator, is a country with a rich biodiversity and cultural heritage. Ecuadorians are proud of their indigenous roots and celebrate them through traditional festivals and crafts like weaving and pottery. The country is also home to the stunning Galapagos Islands, which are famous for their unique wildlife.

Finally, Guatemala is a country with a strong Mayan heritage and a diverse landscape of volcanoes, lakes, and rainforests. Guatemalans are passionate about their traditional textiles and crafts, with many indigenous communities still practicing ancient techniques. The country is also known for its coffee production and vibrant celebrations like Semana Santa and Día de los Muertos.

HOW SPANISH-SPEAKING COUNTRIES VARY

Are you ready to spice up your Spanish? Well, one of the most intriguing things about the Spanish language is the incredible variety of accents and dialects that exist across the world. Just like in English, there are countless ways to say the same thing in Spanish. But don't worry, I'll guide you through some of the most famous ones!

First up, we have the Spanish accent, also known as Castilian Spanish. This is the standard accent used in Spain and is characterized by its crisp, clear pronunciation and its use of the "th" sound instead of the "s" sound for the letters "c" and "z." Some famous local words and expressions include:

- Vale (bah-leh): Okay
- Tío/Tía (tee-oh/tee-ah): Dude/girl
- Me mola (meh moh-lah): I like it
- Estar en el quinto pino (ehs-tahr ehn el keen-toh pee-noh): To be in the middle of nowhere
- Ponerse las botas (poh-nehr-seh lahs boh-tahs): To have a great meal

Next, we have the Mexican accent, which is perhaps the most well-known Spanish accent in the world due to Mexico's cultural influence. The Mexican accent is known for its singsong quality, with a rising intonation at the end of sentences. Some famous local words and expressions include:

- Chido (chee-doh): Cool
- Padre (pah-dreh): Awesome
- Chamba (chahm-bah): Job/work
- Qué onda (keh ohn-dah): What's up?
- Güey (wey): Dude

Moving on to South America, we have the Argentine accent, which is characterized by its distinct "sh" sound for the letters "ll" and "y." The Argentine accent is also known for its use of local slang and expressions. Some famous local words and expressions include:

- Che (cheh): Hey/dude
- Laburar (lah-boo-rahr): To work
- Bárbaro (bar-bah-roh): Great/awesome
- ¿Qué onda? (keh ohn-dah): What's up?
- Boludo/a (boh-loo-doh/boh-loo-dah): Fool/dude

In Colombia, we have the "paisa" accent, which is spoken in the Antioquia region and is known for its soft, melodious sound. Some famous local words and expressions include:

- Parcero/a (pahr-seh-roh/pahr-seh-rah): Friend/buddy
- Chimba (cheem-bah): Cool/awesome
- ¡Quihubo! (kee-oo-boh): What's up?
- Chévere (cheh-veh-reh): Great/cool
- Parche (pahr-cheh): Group of friends/hangout

For many of those who have learned neutral Spanish, the easiest Hispanic accent to identify, but the most difficult to learn, is Chilean. this accent is characterized by being very fast, sung, and closed, but it is also very fun and rhythmic! Some famous local words and expressions include:

- Pololo/a (poh-loh-loh/poh-loh-lah): Boyfriend/girlfriend

- Cachai (kah-chai): Do you understand?
- Bacán (bah-kan): Cool/awesome
- ¡Qué heavy! (keh heh-vee): That's tough/heavy
- Andar al lote (ahn-dahr ahl loh-teh): To be lost/confused

As you can see, the world of Spanish accents and dialects is rich and diverse, reflecting the unique cultural and linguistic traditions of each region. Whether you're learning Spanish for travel, business, or personal enrichment, taking the time to explore the different accents and expressions will deepen your understanding and appreciation of this beautiful language.

In conclusion, each Spanish-speaking country has its unique cultural identity and traditions. Whether you're exploring the bustling markets of Mexico or the stunning landscapes of Peru, there's always something new and exciting to discover.

TIPS ON NAVIGATING CULTURAL DIFFERENCES

As much as we love to travel and learn about new cultures, it's easy to unintentionally offend people when we don't understand their customs. But don't worry, with a little bit of knowledge and effort, you can avoid those uncomfortable situations. Let's go over some dos and don'ts when navigating cultural differences.

Dos:

- Research the culture before you go. This will help you understand the customs, values, and beliefs of the people you will be interacting with.
- Be respectful and open-minded. Show an interest in learning about the culture and be willing to adapt to their way of life.
- Learn some key phrases in their language. This will show that you are making an effort to communicate with them and they will appreciate it.
- Get familiar with greetings and formalities: In many Latin American countries, greetings and formalities are highly valued. Failing to greet someone properly, such as not saying "buenos días" (good morning) or "mucho gusto" (nice to meet you) when appropriate, can be seen as impolite or aloof.
- Dress appropriately. Some cultures have more conservative dress codes than others.
- Be aware of your body language. Gestures that are considered normal in your culture may be offensive to others.

Don'ts:

- Assume everyone speaks English. It's always a good idea to learn some basic words and phrases in the local language.

- Make assumptions about their culture based on stereotypes. Every culture is unique and diverse.
- Bring up politics or religion unless you know the person's point of view. These topics can be sensitive and should be approached with caution.
- Criticize their way of life or customs. Remember, you are a guest in their country.
- Be loud and obnoxious. Some cultures value quietness and restraint.
- Touch someone without permission. Personal space varies from culture to culture.

When it comes to Spanish culture, it's important to be aware of their history and traditions. While Catalonia and Franco may be fascinating topics to you, it's best to avoid discussing them unless you know the person's stance. And, as the majority of Latin Americans are Catholic, it's important to be respectful of their religion. By following these dos and don'ts, you can navigate cultural differences with confidence and respect. ¡Buen viaje!

GETTING GOOD AT CULTURAL IMMERSION

Are you planning to travel to Spain or Latin America soon? Well, it's not just about speaking the language fluently; it's also about immersing yourself in the culture. So, how do you become a master of cultural immersion? Fear not, I've got you covered!

First and foremost, try new foods! Spain is known for its culinary delights, so dive right in! Why not try cooking up some traditional dishes from Peru? Not only will your taste buds be grateful, but you'll also gain a deeper appreciation for the history and culture behind the food.

Next up, explore local customs. Argentina is famous for its tango dancing and mate drinking, so why not give it a try? By doing so, you'll acquire insight into the cultural values and traditions of the people.

Socializing with the locals is also a key component of cultural immersion. Take Bolivia, for example, where people are known for their hospitality and warmth. Strike up a conversation with a local and you might even make a new friend!

To really get a feel for the country, travel to different areas, even the lesser-known ones. Chile is a prime example, with its diverse landscapes ranging from deserts to glaciers. This way, you'll not only experience the beauty of the country but also learn about the history and culture of each region.

Attending live events is another great way to immerse yourself in the culture. In Colombia, for example, the Carnaval de Barranquilla is a must-see event that showcases the country's music, dance, and art.

Don't forget to keep up with the local news, as it will help you understand current events and trends. And if you're really serious about getting involved, why not volunteer with local communities or Spanish-speaking charities in your area? Not only will you be helping others, but you'll also be improving your language skills and gaining a deeper understanding of the culture. It's a win-win situation!

So, there you have it! By following these tips, you'll soon become a master of cultural immersion. Now, grab your passport, and let's go explore!

PRACTICE AND VOCABULARY

1- Read the following story about Álex and answer the questions below:

¿Te imaginas recorrer el continente americano en bicicleta? Pues Álex, un joven aventurero de Ohio, lo hizo posible. Empezando desde su ciudad natal, se adentró en una ruta emocionante hacia el sur de América, y en tan solo 24 meses conoció 11 países, ¡sí, leíste bien, 11 países!

Desde Panamá hasta Argentina, pasando por México, Honduras, Venezuela, Colombia, Brasil, Ecuador, Perú, Bolivia y Chile, Álex no dejó de maravillarse con cada lugar que visitaba. Los desiertos andinos y la fauna patagónica lo dejaron sin aliento, y no podemos culparlo, ¡es que son impresionantes!

Pero eso no es todo, el vasto mar peruano y las ruinas incas lo enamoraron aún más. Además, se aventuró a explorar la espesa selva amazónica de Colombia y a nadar en las aguas tropicales de Venezuela.

Y no solo aprendió a hablar español con fluidez, sino que también descubrió la cultura hispana de primera mano. Al volver a Ohio, se dio cuenta de que lo más valioso que había adquirido en su viaje no fue solo el idioma, sino la apreciación por todas las personas, los lugares, los sabores, los aromas y la música local.

Álex entendió que ese viaje lo había transformado en una persona mucho más tolerante y sencilla, capaz de disfrutar de las pequeñas cosas y valorar cada gesto auténtico. ¡Qué gran lección para todos nosotros!

Ahora mismo él sigue viviendo en su ciudad de origen, y está trabajando duro, pues tiene que ahorrar dinero para su próximo viaje por el mundo. El próximo destino será Japón. Por supuesto, allá no hablan español, asi que Alex tendrá que aprender un nuevo idioma.

¿Quién se anima a seguir los pasos de Álex y explorar el mundo con una mente abierta y un corazón aventurero?

Questions:

1. ¿De dónde es Álex? (Where is Alex from?)
2. ¿Por cuánto tiempo recorrió América del Sur en bicicleta? (For how long did he travel South America by bicycle?)

3. ¿Qué países visitó Álex en su viaje? (Which countries did Alex visit on his trip?)
4. ¿Qué paisajes naturales y sitios históricos visitó Álex durante su viaje? (What natural landscapes and historic sites did Alex visit during his trip?)
5. ¿Qué idioma aprendió Álex durante su viaje? (What language did Alex learn during his trip?)
6. ¿Cómo describirías la actitud de Álex hacia la cultura hispana después de su viaje? (How would you describe Alex's attitude towards Hispanic culture after his trip?)
7. ¿Cómo influyó el viaje de Álex en su personalidad y perspectiva de la vida? (How did Alex's trip influence his personality and perspective on life?)
8. ¿Cómo se sintió Álex al regresar a su hogar en Ohio después de su viaje? (How did Alex feel upon returning to his home in Ohio after his trip?)
9. ¿Dónde vive Alex actualmente y qué esta haciendo allí? ¿Por qué? (Where does Alex currently live and what is he doing there? Why?)
10. ¿Qué tendrá que hacer Alex en su próximo viaje? (What will Alex have to do on his next trip?)

Answers:

1. Álex es de Ohio. (Alex is from Ohio.)
2. Álex recorrió América del Sur en bicicleta durante 24 meses. (Alex traveled South America by bicycle for 24 months.)
3. Álex visitó Panamá, México, Honduras, Colombia, Venezuela, Brasil, Ecuador, Perú, Bolivia, Chile y Argentina en su viaje. (Alex visited Panama, Mexico, Honduras, Colombia, Venezuela, Brazil, Ecuador, Peru, Bolivia, Chile, and Argentina on his trip.)
4. Álex visitó una variedad de paisajes naturales como los desiertos andinos, la fauna patagónica, el vasto mar peruano, las ruinas incas, la selva amazónica de Colombia y las aguas tropicales de Venezuela. (Alex visited a variety of natural landscapes such as the Andean deserts, Patagonian fauna, the vast Peruvian sea, Incan ruins, the Colombian Amazon rainforest, and the tropical waters of Venezuela.)
5. Álex aprendió español durante su viaje. (Alex learned Spanish during his trip.)
6. Después de su viaje, Álex mostró una actitud de aprecio y disfrute hacia la cultura hispana. (After his trip, Alex showed an attitude of appreciation and enjoyment towards Hispanic culture.)
7. El viaje de Álex influyó en su personalidad haciéndolo más tolerante, simple y capaz de valorar las pequeñas cosas y los gestos auténticos. (Alex's trip

influenced his personality, making him more tolerant, simple, and able to value the small things and authentic gestures.)
8. Álex se sintió cambiado y transformado después de su viaje, y se dio cuenta de que había ganado una perspectiva más amplia y apreciativa de la vida. (Alex felt changed and transformed after his trip, realizing that he had gained a broader and appreciative perspective on life.)
9. Álex vive en Ohio y está trabajando duro para ahorrar dinero para su próximo viaje. (Alex lives in Ohio and is working hard to save money for his next trip.)
10. Álex tendrá que aprender un nuevo idioma en Japón. (Alex will have to learn a new language in Japan.)

2- Write the name of the country whose dialect the following phrases belong to:

1. Vale tío, vamos a ponernos las botas en ese restaurante nuevo que me mola. (Okay man, let's get our boots on at that new restaurant that I love.)

_____

2. ¿Qué onda güey? La chamba está muy padre hoy. (What's up dude? The job is really awesome today.)

_____

3. ¡Bárbaro! Mañana voy a laburar desde casa, ¿qué onda con vos? (Great! Tomorrow I'm going to work from home, what's up with you?)

_____

4. ¡Quihubo parcero, que chimba que pudimos salir hoy en parche, estuvo chévere! (What's up friend, it was awesome that we could go out today with the group of friends, it was great!)

_____

5. Estuvimos en el quinto pino para llegar al concierto, pero valió la pena. (We were in the boondocks to get to the concert, but it was worth it.)

_____

6. Mi pololo es bacán y siempre me dice "cachai" cuando hablamos, aunque a veces me ando al lote y no le entiendo bien. (My boyfriend is cool and always says "do you under-

stand?" when we talk, although sometimes I get lost and don't understand him well.)

_____

7. ¡Che boludo, qué onda! Vamos a laburar juntos hoy. (Hey dude, what's up! Let's work together today.)

_____

8. La música de esta fiesta está muy chida, güey. (The music at this party is very cool, dude.)

_____

Answers:

1. Spain
2. Mexico
3. Argentina
4. Colombia
5. Spain
6. Chile
7. Argentina
8. Mexico

Final advice and recommendations:

- Maximize the digital world and available Spanish to improve your language skills.
- Read online Spanish newspapers like El País, 8 Columnas, and El Diario.
- Switch the language of your favorite TV series to Spanish, choosing one with everyday language rather than technical vocabulary. *Friends* is a great option!
- Order in Spanish at your favorite Spanish restaurant and use the language as much as possible.
- Join Spanish language exchange groups on social media or apps like Tandem or HelloTalk to practice with native speakers.

The more you expose yourself to the language, the more you'll improve. Enjoy this whole new world you just discovered ¡Buena suerte, y hasta pronto!

BONUS: THE ULTIMATE SECRET TO MASTERING SPANISH PRONUNCIATION

Learning to speak Spanish fluently is a great accomplishment for anyone who wishes to expand their cultural horizons and connect with millions of people around the world. However, for many English speakers, mastering Spanish pronunciation is a daunting challenge. In this bonus section, I will provide you with a comprehensive guide to help you achieve perfect pronunciation for your Spanish.

As we already learned in the first chapter, Spanish and English share many consonant sounds, but there are five sounds that are always hard for English speakers to master. Let me briefly remind you of them:

1. **The letter "h":** This one is always silent, which can be confusing for English speakers who are used to

pronouncing it. For example, the word "hola" is pronounced as "ola" in Spanish.

2. **The letter "j"**: Its sound is similar to the "h" sound in English, but it is pronounced further back in the throat. To produce the sound, try saying the English "h" sound while exhaling sharply, like a mad cat. For example, the word "joven" is pronounced as "ho-ven" in Spanish.

3. **The letter "ñ"**: The "ñ" is a whole new world for non-native Spanish speakers since its sound does not exist in English, and can be difficult for English speakers to master. To produce the sound, try saying English words like "canyon." The sound made up by the "ny" is quite similar to the Spanish "ñ." For example, the word "niño" is pronounced as "nee-nyo" in Spanish.

4. **The letters "ll" and "y"**: As I mentioned only briefly in the first chapter, in some Spanish-speaking countries, the "ll" sound is pronounced as a "y" sound, while in others they are pronounced as a "sh" sound. Nevertheless, you will have to choose a unique Spanish accent to learn their proper pronunciation. Yet, I will remind you of the sound for "ll" and "y" in neutral Spanish. So, to produce this sound, just do it in the same way you would pronounce "y" in English; For example, the word "lluvia" (rain) is pronounced as "you-via" in Spanish. In the same way, "yema" (bud) is pronounced (yeh-mah).

5. **The letter "r":** In Spanish, the "r" is pronounced with a single tap or flap of the tongue against the roof of the mouth, just behind the front teeth. This is called an alveolar flap or trill, and it produces a distinctive rolling sound. For example, "perro" (dog) is pronounced as "peh-rro" with a trilled "r" sound. In English, the sound of the letter "r" is much softer. Think of the word "pearl" or "ride"; the tip of your tongue never touches the palate, therefore the characteristic vibration of the rolling "r" of Spanish is not produced.

Moving forward, Spanish vowels are relatively easy to pronounce, but some differences between English and Spanish vowel sounds can certainly confuse you. Here are some tips for getting the Spanish vowel sounds right:

1. **The letter "a":** This vowel is always pronounced as "ah," as in "father." For example, the word "casa" is pronounced as "cah-sa."
2. **The letter "e":** It's pronounced as "eh," as in "let." For example, the word "mesa" is pronounced as "meh-sa."
3. **The letter "i":** Must be pronounced as "ee," as in "meet." For example, the word "hijo" is pronounced as "ee-ho" in Spanish.
4. **The letter "o":** This one sounds like the "o" in the English word "go." For example, the word "hola" is pronounced "oh-la."

5. **The letter "u":** Must be pronounced like the "oo" in "moon." For example, the word "uno" is pronounced "oo-no." This vowel is particularly difficult for English speakers because its Spanish sound does not exist in English. That is, there is a similar sound—like the "oo" in "moon"—but it is not the same. While in English the sound "oo" comes from the throat, in Spanish it is achieved by bringing the lips forward and slightly squeezing them, leaving a small space to let the air out of the mouth—similar to how we would do it when whistling or giving a kiss.

Spanish pronunciation is relatively simple and straightforward compared to many other languages. Unlike many languages where spelling and pronunciation are not always consistent, Spanish is a phonetic language, meaning that words are pronounced as they are written. This is a major advantage for language learners and the ultimate secret to mastering Spanish pronunciation I promised you: **Once you master the sounds of each letter of the Spanish alphabet, you will be able to read and pronounce all the words in Spanish correctly.**

One of the primary reasons for this is that Spanish has a relatively small number of phonemes (distinct sounds), making it easier to learn than languages with larger phonemic inventories. In contrast, picture this: Mandarin Chinese has about 420 sounds, including consonants, vowels, and diphthongs (Encyclopedia Britannica., n.d.).

In Spanish, there are only five vowel sounds, while in English, there are more than ten. Additionally, Spanish has fewer consonant sounds than English, which further simplifies the language.

Another factor that makes Spanish pronunciation easier to master is that many of the sounds in Spanish are similar to those in English. For example, the Spanish "b" and "v" sounds are identical or very similar to the English "b" sound.

One of the biggest fears that language learners have is not sounding like a native speaker. And this applies to all people who speak a second language, not just to Spanish amateurs. While it's certainly true that mastering a foreign language's pronunciation takes time and practice, it's also important to remember that having an accent is not necessarily a bad thing.

Accents are a natural part of language diversity, and they reflect a person's unique background and linguistic history.

Moreover, learning a new language is an achievement in itself, regardless of whether you sound like a native speaker or not. The goal of language learning should be effective communication, not necessarily achieving native-like fluency. It's worth remembering that most native Spanish speakers will be impressed that you've made the effort to learn their language, regardless of whether you have an accent or not.

It's important to embrace your accent and make it part of your linguistic identity. It can be a nice or distinctive trait rather than a liability, as it can make you stand out and add to the diversity of the communities you're part of. So, don't be discouraged by the prospect of not sounding like a native speaker; embrace your unique voice and celebrate your love for the Spanish language!

BONUS: PRACTICE AND VOCABULARY

1- Learn new tenses to expand your knowledge of Spanish to the highest level. Observe the explanation and its examples.

a. Preterite Perfect and Imperfect:

In Spanish, the preterite perfect (also known as past simple) and imperfect are both past tenses, but they have different uses. The preterite perfect is used to describe completed actions in the recent past, while the imperfect is used to describe ongoing or habitual actions in the past.

Here is a table with the conjugations in all the grammatical persons of 10 verbs in the preterit perfect or past simple tense in Spanish:

Verbo	Yo	Tú	Él/Ella/Usted	Nosotros/Nosotras	Vosotros/Vosotras	Ellos/Ellas/Ustedes
Salir	Salí	Saliste	Salió	Salimos	Salisteis	Salieron
Escapar	Escapé	Escapaste	Escapó	Escapamos	Escapasteis	Escaparon
Comer	Comí	Comiste	Comió	Comimos	Comisteis	Comieron
Hablar	Hablé	Hablaste	Habló	Hablamos	Hablasteis	Hablaron
Caminar	Caminé	Caminaste	Caminó	Caminamos	Caminasteis	Caminaron
Correr	Corrí	Corriste	Corrió	Corrimos	Corristeis	Corrieron
Vivir	Viví	Viviste	Vivió	Vivimos	Vivisteis	Vivieron
Llegar	Llegué	Llegaste	Llegó	Llegamos	Llegasteis	Llegaron
Tomar	Tomé	Tomaste	Tomó	Tomamos	Tomasteis	Tomaron
Cantar	Canté	Cantaste	Cantó	Cantamos	Cantasteis	Cantaron

For example:

- Después de que ella terminó de estudiar, se fue a la cama. (After she finished studying, she went to bed.)
- Cuando él recibió la noticia, sintió una gran alegría. (When he received the news, he felt a great joy.)

- A pesar de que llovió todo el día, disfrutamos de nuestras vacaciones. (Although it rained all day, we enjoyed our vacation.)
- Tan pronto como ellos llegaron a la playa, se quitaron los zapatos. (As soon as they arrived at the beach, they took off their shoes.)
- Una vez que terminaron de cocinar, comenzaron a preparar la mesa. (Once they finished cooking, they started setting the table.)

Now, I present the same list but with these conjugated verbs in the imperfect past tense of Spanish:

Verbo	Yo	Tú	Él/Ella/Usted	Nosotros/Nosotras	Vosotro/Vosotras	Ellos/Ellas/Ustedes
Salir	Salía	Salías	Salía	Salíamos	Salíais	Salían
Escapar	Escapaba	Escapabas	Escapaba	Escapábamos	Escapabais	Escapaban
Comer	Comía	Comías	Comía	Comíamos	Comíais	Comían
Hablar	Hablaba	Hablabas	Hablaba	Hablábamos	Hablabais	Hablaban
Caminar	Caminaba	Caminabas	Caminaba	Caminábamos	Caminabais	Caminaban
Correr	Corría	Corrías	Corría	Corríamos	Corríais	Corrían
Vivir	Vivía	Vivías	Vivía	Vivíamos	Vivíais	Vivían
Llegar	Llegaba	Llegabas	Llegaba	Llegábamos	Llegabais	Llegaban
Tomar	Tomaba	Tomabas	Tomaba	Tomábamos	Tomabais	Tomaban
Cantar	Cantaba	Cantabas	Cantaba	Cantábamos	Cantabais	Cantaban

For example:

- Cuando era niño, siempre jugaba al fútbol con mis amigos del barrio. (When I was a child, I always used to play soccer with my friends from the neighborhood.)
- Mientras estudiábamos para el examen, nos dimos cuenta de que nos faltaba un libro importante. (While we were studying for the exam, we realized that we were missing an important book.)
- A pesar de que llovía, la gente seguía haciendo compras en el mercado. (Despite the fact that it was raining, people kept shopping at the market.)
- Cuando vivía en Nueva York, iba al cine todos los fines de semana. (When I lived in New York, I used to go to the movies every weekend.)
- Mientras preparábamos la cena, escuchábamos música en la radio. (While we were preparing dinner, we were listening to music on the radio.)

b. Future Conditional:

The future conditional in Spanish is a tense that is used to talk about hypothetical actions that could happen in the future, but that depend on a previous condition. For example, in the sentence "Si tuviera más dinero, viajaría por todo el mundo" (If I had more money, I would travel around the world), the verb "viajaría" (I would travel) is in the future conditional, since it indicates a hypothetical action that would only occur if the condition of having more money is met.

The future conditional can also be used to express a wish or a request in a more polite way. For example, in the sentence "I would like to go to the movies tonight," the verb "would like" is in the future conditional and is used to express a wish in a more polite way.

Here is a table with the conjugations in all the grammatical persons in some future conditional verbs in Spanish:

Verbo	Yo	Tú	Él/Ella/Usted	Nosotros/Nosotras	Vosotro/Vosotras	Ellos/Ellas/Ustedes
Tener	Tendría	Tendrías	Tendría	Tendríamos	Tendríais	Tendrían
Poder	Podría	Podrías	Podría	Podríamos	Podríais	Podrían
Saber	Sabría	Sabrías	Sabría	Sabríamos	Sabríais	Sabrían
Querer	Querría	Querrías	Querría	Querríamos	Querríais	Querrían
Hacer	Haría	Harías	Haría	Haríamos	Haríais	Harían
Decir	Diría	Dirías	Diría	Diríamos	Diríais	Dirían
Ir	Iría	Irías	Iría	Iríamos	Iríais	Irían
Venir	Vendría	Vendrías	Vendría	Vendríamos	Vendríais	Vendrían
Ser	Sería	Serías	Sería	Seríamos	Seríais	Serían
Estar	Estaría	Estarías	Estaría	Estaríamos	Estaríais	Estarían

Examples:

- Si tuviera más tiempo, me gustaría aprender a tocar el piano. (If I had more time, I would like to learn how to play the piano.)
- Si pudiera hablar francés, viajaría a París sin dudarlo. (If I could speak French, I would travel to Paris without hesitation.)
- Si supiera la respuesta, te ayudaría con el problema. (If I knew the answer, I would help you with the problem.)
- Si quisieras venir conmigo, te mostraría mi ciudad favorita. (If you wanted to come with me, I would show you my favorite city.)
- Si fuera millonario, donaría una parte de mi dinero a obras benéficas. (If I were a millionaire, I would donate a portion of my money to charitable causes.)

2- Put these new tenses into practice:

a. Write a short biography of a famous person in Spanish, using the past perfect or simple tense to talk about their achievements and important events in their life.

For example: Julio César **fue** un político romano. **Nació** en Roma, **creció** y **estudió** allí hasta que **cumplió** la mayoría de edad… (Julius Caesar was a Roman politician. He was born in Rome, grew up and studied there until he came of age…)

b. Complete the following sentences with the correct form of the past perfect (or simple) of the verb in parentheses:

1. Yo _____ (comprar) un regalo para mi mamá.
2. Ellos _____ (viajar) por Europa el verano pasado.
3. Tú _____ (estudiar) mucho para el examen.
4. Él _____ (escribir) una novela el año pasado.
5. Nosotros _____ (aprender) a tocar la guitarra en el conservatorio.
6. Vosotros _____ (hacer) una cena deliciosa para vuestros amigos.
7. Ella _____ (visitar) a su familia en Navidad.
8. Ustedes _____ (ver) la película en el cine anoche.

Answers:

1. compré
2. viajaron
3. estudiaste
4. escribió
5. aprendimos
6. hicísteis
7. visitó
8. vieron

c. Create a story in which you use the imperfect tense to describe the scenes, characters, and actions that occurred.

For example: **Había** una vez un león llamado Magnus. Él **estaba** muy hambriento y **esperaba** tras un arbusto por su presa… (Once upon a time there was a lion named Magnus. He was very hungry and waited behind a bush for his prey…)

_____

_____

d. Write a list of 10 things you would do if you had an extra day off. Use the conditional to describe the activities you would like to do.

For example: Si no **tuviera** que trabajar el domingo, **iría** a conocer el nuevo acuario de la ciudad. (If I didn't have to work on Sunday, I'd go to see the new aquarium in town.)

1. _____
2. _____
3. _____
4. _____
5. _____
6. _____
7. _____
8. _____
9. _____

CONCLUSION

Learning a new language is a journey that requires dedication, effort, and patience. I commend you for committing yourself to this adventure, and for taking the time to invest in your personal development. Learning Spanish—like any other new language—will open up doors to new opportunities, whether it be for travel, work, and, who knows, maybe love—as was my case!

We started this journey together by discussing the benefits of learning Spanish, including the ability to communicate with millions of people all over the world. The first chapter of this book focused on the Spanish alphabet and pronunciation. I have provided a guide to the sounds and letters of the Spanish language, as well as tips and tricks for mastering the pronunciation, funny useful exercises and vocabulary lists to help you practice and build your skills at the bottom of every chapter.

Chapter 2 focused on essential Spanish vocabulary. We covered keywords and phrases that you're likely to encounter in everyday conversations that will allow you to describe objects, housework, name animals, professions, and hobbies, among other things.

Later, in Chapter 3, we turned our attention to numbers and time. We covered how to tell time in Spanish, as well as how to count and use numbers in various contexts.

In Chapter 4, we focused on common words and phrases for everyday situations. We addressed topics such as greetings and introductions, ordering food at a restaurant, expressing likes and dislikes, and making small talk.

Chapter 5 delved into Spanish grammar. We covered important grammatical concepts such as gender, singular and plural forms, and sentence structure.

Moving on to Chapter 6, we emphasized the importance of verbs in Spanish. We learned how to conjugate regular and irregular verbs, as well as how to use verbs in different tenses.

The last chapter focused on Spanish culture and customs. It brought you an overview of the rich history and traditions of the Spanish-speaking world, as well as tips and insights for navigating cultural differences. Finally, I told you an exciting story about a bike traveler that I strongly encourage you to read over and over again.

Finally, in the Bonus chapter, I shared with you the ultimate secret to mastering Spanish pronunciation by showing you additional tips and exercises to help you fine-tune your pronunciation and build your confidence in speaking Spanish. By the end, we also talked about the importance of not being ashamed of our foreign accent when speaking Spanish or any other second language, since it is nothing more than part of our identity.

It is necessary to reinforce what you have learned so far so that it sticks in your memory. Remember to use multiple learning techniques such as flashcards, recording your own voice, making mind maps, labeling items in your home, and speaking to yourself in the mirror. Immerse yourself in Spanish-speaking environments, listen to Spanish music and watch Spanish films, and engage in conversations with native speakers. The more you expose yourself to the language, the more comfortable and confident you will become. These techniques may seem silly at first, but they are proven to be effective in reinforcing learning and retaining information.

I want to take this opportunity to share my own success story with you. As a native Spanish speaker who had to learn English, I can confidently say that learning a new language can be challenging but also incredibly rewarding. By having English and Spanish as my skill sets, I have been able to travel to so many countries in the world, and have meaningful, interesting conversations with people from different backgrounds. Learning Spanish will open doors to new opportunities and experiences that may have otherwise been unavailable.

As we conclude, I encourage you to take the next steps in your language-learning journey. Incorporate Spanish into your daily life by thinking in Spanish, using Spanish words to navigate your surroundings, and practicing your speaking skills whenever possible. Remember that the more you immerse yourself in the language, the faster you will pick it up.

I would love to read your feedback on this book and how it has helped you in your language-learning journey. Reviews are an important way to share your opinions and experiences to help others who are also interested in learning Spanish. **By leaving a review, you will inspire and encourage others to take the leap and start speaking Spanish themselves.**

Scan the QR Code to leave a review!

Learn Spanish for Adult Beginners: Speak Confidently & Impress Your Amigos has been a comprehensive guide aimed at providing you with everything you need to quickly learn Spanish. If you continue to follow the tips and exercises provided in each chapter, you will undoubtedly build your skills and confidence in speaking and understanding Spanish. I hope that this book has been a valuable resource for you and that it has inspired you to continue learning and exploring the rich and vibrant world of the Spanish language and culture.

¡Gracias y hasta pronto!

REFERENCES

Az Quotes. (n.d.). *Angela Carter quote.* A-Z Quotes. https://www.azquotes.com/quote/611535

Encyclopedia Britannica. (n.d.). *Chinese languages.* https://www.britannica.com/topic/Chinese-languages

Newsdle. (n.d.). *Brief history of Spanish language.* https://www.newsdle.com/blog/brief-history-of-spanish-language#:~:text=Spanish%20originated%20in%20the%20Iberian,spread%20around%20the%20world%20thereafter.

Tell Me In Spanish. (n.d.). *Spanish language statistics.* https://www.tellmeinspanish.com/stats/spanish-language-statistics/

WhyNotSpanish. (2018). *¡Ojalá! The Spanish word with Arabic origins.* https://www.whynotspanish.com/ojala-spanish-word-arabic-origins/

Made in the USA
Las Vegas, NV
09 January 2024

84159393R00132